Amazon Bestselling Author of
The Chausathi Yoginis of Hirapur and The Yoginis of Ranipur Jharial

Forgotten Goddesses

Forgotten Goddesses

Dr. Adyasha Das

BLACK EAGLE BOOKS
Dublin, USA | Bhubaneswar, India

Black Eagle Books
USA address:
7464 Wisdom Lane
Dublin, OH 43016

India address:
E/312, Trident Galaxy, Kalinga Nagar,
Bhubaneswar-751003, Odisha, India

E-mail: info@blackeaglebooks.org
Website: www.blackeaglebooks.org

First International Edition Published by
Black Eagle Books, 2023

FORGOTTEN GODDESSES
by **Dr. Adyasha Das**

Copyright © Dr. Adyasha Das

All rights reserved. No part of this publication may be reproduced, stored in a retrieval system, or transmitted, in any form or by any means, electronic, mechanical, photocopying, recording or otherwise without the prior permission of the publisher.

Cover photo: *Sculpture of Goddess Cunda- The British Museum*

Cover & Interior Design: Ezy's Publication

ISBN- 978-1-64560-462-4 (Paperback)
Library of Congress Control Number: 2023949073

Printed in the United States of America

"To the timeless and forgotten goddesses - in reverence and remembrance."

Contents

Preface	09
Chapter 1	
Introduction	15
Chapter 2	
Evolution of the Goddess	38
Chapter 3	
Forgotten Goddesses	56
Chapter 4	
The Dasamahavidyas	110
Chapter 5	
Grama Devatas/Grama Devatis of Odisha	135
Chapter 6	
Malevolent Goddesses	164
Chapter 7	
Goddesses of Tribal Shamanism in Different Parts of India	169
Chapter 8	
Goddess Yakshi	172
Chapter 9	
Pillar Goddesses	174
Chapter 10	
Chausathi Yoginis of Hirapur	177
Chapter 11	
The Chausathi Yoginis of Ranipur Jharial	200
References	219

PREFACE

In the tapestry of human history, there exists a rich and intricate thread woven by the belief in the divine feminine. Across cultures, civilizations, and epochs, the concept of the Goddess has played a pivotal role in shaping the spiritual and cultural landscape of our world. Her influence is omnipresent, touching every aspect of our lives, from the natural world to the profound mysteries of creation. In this book, we embark on a journey to rediscover the Forgotten Goddesses, those divine feminine beings who have been overshadowed by more prominent deities, yet whose stories and wisdom hold timeless significance.

The notion of the Goddess is an integral part of human spirituality. In the realm of the divine, she represents the nurturing, creative, and regenerative forces that underlie the universe. She is the embodiment of the Earth, the Moon, the stars, and the waters. Her presence is found in the cycles of nature, the flow of time, and the depths of our collective unconscious. This divine feminine principle has been recognized and celebrated in myriad ways throughout history.

One of the most captivating aspects of the Goddess concept is its universality. Across continents and cultures, people have revered a feminine deity or pantheon, each with unique characteristics and attributes. In ancient

Mesopotamia, there was Inanna, the Queen of Heaven, who presided over love, fertility, and war. The Greeks worshipped Athena, the wise goddess of wisdom and strategy, while the Romans venerated Minerva, her counterpart. In the Norse tradition, Freyja was the goddess of love, beauty, and fertility, while in ancient Egypt, Isis was revered as a mother goddess and protector of the dead. These are just a few examples of the diverse and multifaceted ways in which the divine feminine has been celebrated around the world.

In the Indian subcontinent, the concept of the Goddess holds a particularly prominent place in spiritual and cultural life. India is a land where the divine feminine is not just a belief but a living reality. It is a place where Goddess worship is deeply ingrained in the fabric of society, where millions of devotees seek solace and strength in the Mother Goddess, Devi. From the fierce Durga who battles the forces of evil, to the gentle Parvati who embodies love and devotion, the pantheon of Hindu goddesses is vast and enchanting.

Moreover, India's spiritual landscape has nurtured the concept of Shakti, the primordial cosmic energy, which is personified as the Divine Mother. This recognition of the Goddess as the source of all energy and power has profound implications for the understanding of the universe and the self. The Indian tradition is replete with stories, rituals, and practices that celebrate the divine feminine in all her forms. It is a tradition that extends far beyond the borders of India and resonates with people worldwide who are drawn to the depth and beauty of the Goddess concept.

Despite the global prevalence of the Goddess in human history, many of her aspects and incarnations have been forgotten, overshadowed, or marginalized over time. This book is a journey of rekindling the lost stories of these Forgotten Goddesses. It is a celebration of the divine feminine in all its manifestations, an exploration of the archetypes that have shaped human spirituality, and an invitation to embrace the sacred feminine within ourselves.

The divine feminine is not just a relic of the past, but a living force that continues to inspire and empower people today. In an era where gender equality and the reclamation of women's voices are at the forefront of social discourse, the Goddess offers a unique perspective on spirituality that is inclusive, empowering, and transcendent of traditional gender roles. She calls us to honour and respect the feminine qualities within ourselves and in the world around us, to recognize that balance and harmony between the masculine and the feminine are essential for the well-being of our planet.

Throughout this book, we will delve into the stories, myths, and rituals associated with Forgotten Goddesses from various cultures, while also paying special attention to the enduring influence of the divine feminine in India and Odisha. The book explores the concept of the Goddess as a symbol of nature, creativity, and transformation. We will unravel her connection to fertility, life, death, and rebirth.

As we embark on this journey of rediscovery, let us remember that the Forgotten Goddesses have never truly vanished. They have merely retreated into the recesses of our collective memory, waiting for us to rediscover and rekindle their essence. They are here to remind us of the divine feminine within ourselves, to empower us with their wisdom, and to inspire us to embrace the sacred in all of life. In their stories, we find a source of strength, wisdom, and inspiration that transcends time and space. In their worship, we find a pathway to reconnect with the profound mysteries of existence. This book is an invitation to walk this path, to reawaken the presence of the Goddess in our hearts and minds, and to embrace her as a source of empowerment, wisdom, and spiritual illumination. As we delve into the stories and mysteries of the Forgotten Goddesses, may we also uncover the divine feminine within ourselves and in the world around us. For it is in this union of the inner and outer Goddess that we find balance, harmony, and a profound sense of purpose.

I thank Satya Pattanaik, Director, Black Eagle Books, USA for supporting the publication of this book. He has published my books previously and extended his unstinted support for their sustained promotion. Four of my books have made it to the Amazon Bestseller list. I extend my thanks to Ashok Parida, BEB for a beautiful cover design and lay-out.

My thanks go to Sankar Narayan Mallik, who has rendered invaluable help and his expertise in reading the manuscript thoroughly and providing indispensable editorial insights. I thank him for his co-operation in my literary endeavours.

My family, Lalit and Ishani, share my interest for travel and literature. Had it not been for them, my literary endeavours would have been difficult. As a senior police officer, my husband, Lalit Das, ADG, Police, Govt. of Odisha had friends at all these far-flung destinations who have rendered invaluable help to me in the process of my research. Special thanks to my mother, Pratibha Ray, who is in the truest sense, a friend, philosopher and guide, and has been a constructive critic at all times. As a writer herself, my discussions with her in the course of my research and writings were very helpful to me.

I express my heartfelt gratitude to my readers for their unwavering support and enthusiasm for my books. It is with immense joy and appreciation that I acknowledge the fact that your loyal readership has given my books the status of being bestsellers. Your reviews and discussions about my books have provided me with invaluable feedback and inspiration. Your enthusiasm and encouragement have fuelled my creativity and propelled me to keep striving for excellence in every piece of writing I produce.

This book is a collection of experiences of my visits and travels to different temples and temple towns over time in India and abroad. Needless to say, there are many more that will probably run into another volume. My research in the area of cultural and heritage tourism intensified the interest for visiting and understanding spiritual spaces. Most of the photographs are mine and some belong to my dear students. Few have been chosen from the internet.

Religions have extolled women as rendering dominant roles in leadership and creative inventions of cultures. Mostly, I pay reverence to the unseen force which made me know the world in myself through the visits to temples and Goddesses.

Chapter 1

Introduction

Forgotten Goddesses

The concept of a goddess or supreme power has a rich and diverse history that spans cultures and civilizations across the world. In Hinduism, the origins of the goddess concept can be traced back to the ancient Indus Valley Civilization, which existed around 2500-1500 BCE However, it is important to note that the understanding of goddesses and the concept of a supreme power can vary within different sects and traditions of Hinduism.

In the Indus Valley Civilization, archaeological evidence suggests the existence of a mother goddess figure. Various terracotta figurines and seals depicting a feminine deity have been discovered at Indus Valley sites such as Harappa and Mohenjo-Daro. These representations indicate the worship of a female divinity associated with fertility, nurturing, and protection.Moving forward in history, the Vedic period (1500-500 BCE) played a significant role in shaping the concept of goddesses in Hinduism. The Vedas, the oldest sacred texts of Hinduism, contain hymns and prayers dedicated to various deities, both male and female. In this period, deities such as Ushas (the goddess of dawn) and Saraswati (the goddess of knowledge and learning) were revered.

The rise of the devotional and philosophical movements during the medieval period further contributed to the development of the goddess concept. The Bhakti movement, which emerged around the 6th century CE, emphasized intense personal devotion to a chosen deity, and this devotion was often directed towards goddesses. Prominent female deities like Durga, Kali, Lakshmi, and Parvati gained significant importance during this time.

The concept of Shakti, the divine feminine energy or power, also became central to Hindu thought and theology. Shakti is believed to be the dynamic force that permeates the entire universe and manifests in various goddess forms. This concept found expression in the Devi Mahatmya (also known as Durga Saptashati or Chandi), a scripture composed around the 5th century CE. It narrates the stories of the goddess Durga's battles against various demons and her ultimate victory, symbolizing the triumph of good over evil. The Devī Māhātmya ('Glorification of the Goddess') embedded in the Mārkaeya Purāa along with the Devī Bhāgavatapurāa, is a fundamental work in Shaktism. This tradition of Hinduism emphasizes that Devī, the Goddess also known as Durgā, is the Supreme all-pervading reality of existence.

(Devi Mahatmya: The British Library)

Devi Mahatmya, also known as Durga Saptashati or Chandi Path, is a sacred text from Hindu mythology that celebrates the divine feminine energy and the victory of the goddess Durga over the demon Mahishasura. It is a significant portion of the larger ancient Indian epic, Markandeya Purana. Comprising 700 verses divided into 13 chapters, the text is revered for its spiritual and ritualistic importance.

Essential points of the Devi Mahatmya:

Origin and Composition: Devi Mahatmya is believed to have been composed around the 5th to 6th centuries CE, though the story and concepts it presents have roots in ancient Hindu mythology. The text is attributed to the sage Markandeya, who narrates the divine story to King Suratha and the merchant Samadhi seeking liberation from their worldly troubles.

The Devi Mahatmya is divided into three sections, each describing the exploits of a different aspect of the goddess Durga:

Prathama Charitra (First Episode): Chapters 1 to 5 focus on the manifestation and divine deeds of Maha Kali, the fierce form of the goddess. They describe how she destroys the demons Madhu-Kaitabha and Mahishasura.

Madhyama Charitra (Middle Episode): Chapters 6 to 9 highlight the stories related to Maha Lakshmi, the goddess of wealth and prosperity. This section includes the slaying of the demon Raktabija and the tale of the demons Shumbha and Nishumbha.

Uttama Charitra (Final Episode): Chapters 10 to 13 centre around Maha Saraswati, the goddess of knowledge and wisdom. The text elaborates how she vanquishes the demon Dhumralochana and the powerful demon brothers, Chanda and Munda.

The Symbolism: Devi Mahatmya is deeply symbolic, and each character and event holds profound meaning. The demons represent various negative qualities such as ego, ignorance, and attachment, while the goddesses represent divine virtues and powers that help overcome these negativities.

Importance of Feminine Energy: The text extols the significance of feminine energy, portraying the goddess as the embodiment of Shakti, the primordial cosmic energy. She is shown as the source of creation, sustenance, and destruction, reflecting the dynamic nature of the universe.

Victory of Good over Evil: Devi Mahatmya celebrates the triumph of good over evil. It emphasizes that whenever evil forces become too dominant and threaten the cosmic order, the divine feminine energy incarnates to restore balance and protect the universe.

Devotional and Ritual Significance: Devi Mahatmya holds immense religious significance in Hindu traditions. It is recited during Navaratri, a nine-day festival dedicated to the worship of the goddess Durga. Devotees believe that chanting or reading the verses brings blessings, protection, and fulfilment of desires.

Verses and Mantras: The verses of Devi Mahatmya are powerful mantras with profound effects. They are chanted for spiritual upliftment, dispelling negativity, and invoking divine blessings. Some of the prominent mantras from the text include the Navarna Mantra (Om Aim Hreem Kleem Chamundaye Viche) and the Devi Kavacham (Armour of the Goddess).

Philosophical and Spiritual Teachings: Along with its devotional aspects, the text contains philosophical and spiritual teachings. It explores concepts like the nature of reality, the interplay of good and evil, the path to liberation (moksha), and the significance of surrendering to the divine.

The idea of a divine feminine principle first appeared in the hymns of the Rig Veda and later in the Upanishads, however the Devī Māhātmya is probably the first text to distinctly present the Goddess manifestation as an object of devotion.

Another significant text associated with goddess worship is the Devi Bhagavata Purana, which focuses on the divine feminine principle. It describes the origins and exploits of various goddesses, including Devi (the supreme goddess), Lakshmi (goddess of wealth and prosperity), and Saraswati (goddess of knowledge and arts).

Arthur Basham, renowned historian wrote:

"The theme of shakti perhaps grew out of a conflict and eventual compromise between a powerful matriarchal culture that existed in India before the Aryan migrations (2500, B.C. [B.C.E.]) and the male-dominated society of the Aryans. The Mother Goddess of the Indus Valley people never really gave place to a dominant male. The Earth Mother continues to be worshipped in India as the power that nurtures the seed and brings it to fruition.

This basic reverence of an agricultural people affirms that man is really dependent on woman for she gives life, food and strength. Mother Goddesses were worshipped at all times in India, but between the days of the Harappa Culture (2500-1500 B.C. [B.C.E.]) and the Gupta period (ca. 300-500) the cults of goddesses attracted little attention from the learned and influential, and only emerged from obscurity to a position of real importance in the

Middle Ages, when feminine divinities, theoretically connected with the gods as their spouses, were once more worshipped by the upper classes...by the Gupta Period the wives of the gods, whose existence had always been recognized, but who had been shadowy figures in earlier theology, began to be worshipped in special temples (Arthur L. Basham, Wonder That Was India Revised Edition [London: Sedgwick& Jackson, 1967], 313)."

Kingsley describes the concept of Shakti in the following words:

"Sakti [shakti] means "power"; in Hindu philosophy and theology sakti is understood to be the active dimension of the godhead, the divine power that underlies the godhead's ability to create the world and to display itself. Within the totality of the godhead, sakti is the complementary pole of the divine tendency toward quiescence and stillness. It is quite common, furthermore, to identify sakti with a female being, a goddess, and to identify the other pole with her male consort. The two poles are usually understood to be interdependent and to have relatively equal status in terms of the divine economy (David R. Kinsley, Hindu Goddesses: Visions of the Divine Feminine in the Hindu Religious Tradition [Berkeley: University of California Press, 1986], 133)."

Shakti symbolizes the dynamic energy instrumental for creation, maintenance, and destruction of the universe. She stimulates Siva, passive energy in the form of consciousness, to create. Ardhanarishvara, Hindu deity (half male and half female), is a unique representation of this idea, illustrating that the creation, maintenance, and destruction of the universe is dependent on both forces.

Shakti also refers to the manifestations of this energy as goddesses. Some goddesses embody the destructive aspects of Shakti, like death, degeneration, and illness, while other goddesses represent the creative and auspicious powers of Shakti, such as nature, the elements, music, art, dance, and prosperity. The personification of Shakti may be as the gentle and generous Uma, or Kali, the aggressive force destroying evil, or Durga, who conquers forces that attempt to destabilize the universe. Goddess worshippers regard their deity as the Supreme Being, second to none, not even to a male god. There are enduring goddess traditions all over India, especially in West Bengal and South India. Goddesses symbolizing different manifestations of power are found to predominate in village culture.

David Kinsley writes:

Texts or contexts exalting the Mahadevi [Great Goddess], however, usually affirm sakti to be a power, or the power, underlying ultimate reality, or to be ultimate reality itself. Instead of being understood as one of two poles or as one dimension of a bipolar conception of the divine, sakti as it applies to the Mahadevi is often identified with the essence of reality (Ibid., 135).

The goddess concept in Hinduism encompasses a wide range of qualities and attributes. Goddesses are often associated with motherhood, fertility, wisdom, power, protection, and divine grace. They are seen as embodiments of feminine energy and serve as symbols of empowerment, compassion, and spiritual enlightenment.It is important to recognize that the understanding and interpretation of goddesses can vary among different Hindu sects and regional traditions. The multifaceted nature of Hinduism allows for a diverse range of goddess worship practices and beliefs, contributing to the richness and complexity of the goddess concept in the religion.

Overall, the origins of the goddess concept in the world and Hinduism can be traced back to ancient civilizations, and it has evolved and been shaped by various historical, cultural, and philosophical influences over time. The worship of goddesses and the recognition of a supreme power in feminine form have played a significant role in shaping Hindu religious and philosophical thought.

The Goddess Movement:

The Goddess Movement is a modern spiritual and cultural movement that emerged in the 1970s and gained popularity in the following decades. It focuses on the reclamation and celebration of the feminine divine, emphasizing the importance of goddesses and female deities from various mythologies and religious traditions.

The movement draws inspiration from ancient goddess-centered cultures, such as those of the Mediterranean region, Mesopotamia, and the Indus Valley Civilization. It seeks to restore the prominence of the feminine divine that has often been marginalized or overshadowed in many mainstream religious traditions, which are predominantly male-centred.

One of the key principles of the Goddess movement is the belief in the immanence of the divine, asserting that the sacred is present in all aspects of life and the natural world. This perspective stands in contrast to the transcendent and patriarchal view of a distant, male God that is prevalent in many monotheistic religions.

The Goddess movement recognizes and celebrates the diversity of the divine feminine by honouring goddesses from various cultures and mythologies. Some of the goddesses commonly revered within the movement include Isis from ancient Egypt, Gaia from Greek mythology, Kali from Hinduism, Brigid from Celtic mythology, and many others. Each goddess is seen as embodying unique qualities and aspects of the feminine divine, such as love, fertility, wisdom, strength, and transformation.

The movement often incorporates rituals, ceremonies, and practices inspired by ancient goddess worship. These may include meditation, chanting, dance, art, and healing ceremonies. Many followers of the Goddess movement engage in personal or group rituals to connect with the divine feminine and to tap into their own inner power and wisdom.

The Goddess movement also places a strong emphasis on environmentalism and the interconnectedness of all living beings. It recognizes the Earth as a sacred entity, often referred to as Mother Earth or Gaia, and advocates for ecological awareness, sustainability, and the preservation of the natural world. The movement sees the degradation of the environment as a result of the patriarchal domination and exploitation of nature, and seeks to restore a balance between humanity and the Earth.

Another important aspect of the Goddess movement is its commitment to promoting women's empowerment and the dismantling of patriarchal systems. It seeks to challenge and transform traditional gender roles and hierarchies that have oppressed and marginalized women. The movement encourages women to embrace their innate power, wisdom, and creativity, and to reclaim their spiritual authority.

The Goddess movement has been influential in inspiring women's spirituality, feminist theology, and new forms of religious expression. It has given rise to the creation of women-only rituals and sacred spaces, the publication of books and magazines exploring goddess spirituality, and the establishment of organizations and communities dedicated to the worship and study of the divine feminine.

It is important to note that the Goddess movement is diverse and decentralized, with various interpretations and practices. Different individuals and groups within the movement may have different emphases, rituals, and beliefs. Some may focus on a specific goddess or pantheon, while others may explore a broader range of goddesses and spiritual traditions.

The movement represents a contemporary response to the perceived imbalance and exclusion of the feminine divine in traditional religious and cultural contexts. It offers a framework for reconnecting with the sacred feminine, celebrating women's spirituality, and fostering social and ecological transformation.

The origins of the first form of worship can be traced back to the early stages of human civilization, when people began to develop a sense of awe and reverence for the natural world and the forces they perceived as beyond their control. As early humans observed the cycles of nature, the movements of celestial bodies, and the power of natural phenomena like thunderstorms and earthquakes, they likely developed a desire to appease and connect with these forces.

In their quest to understand and relate to the divine or supernatural, early humans engaged in various practices that can be considered as rudimentary forms of worship. These practices often involved creating sacred spaces or sanctuaries, offering sacrifices or gifts, and engaging in rituals and ceremonies. These actions were meant to establish a connection with the divine and seek its favour or protection.

The exact reasons why rites and rituals became a part of the worship process are complex and multifaceted.

Several factors could have contributed to their development and proliferation:

Communication and Exchange: Rites and rituals provided a means of communication with the divine or supernatural entities. Early humans believed that through specific actions, words, or gestures, they could establish a connection and convey their desires, gratitude, or supplications.

Symbolism and Representation: Rituals often involve the use of symbols, gestures, and objects that represent or embody the divine or supernatural. These symbolic elements helped early humans conceptualize and interact with abstract concepts and forces that were beyond their immediate comprehension.

Social Cohesion and Identity: Rites and rituals played a significant role in fostering social cohesion and identity within early human communities. Shared religious practices and beliefs helped strengthen social bonds, create a sense of belonging, and establish a collective identity.

Order and Stability: Rituals provided a sense of order, structure, and predictability in a world that early humans perceived as chaotic and unpredictable. Engaging in prescribed actions and following specific rituals helped establish a sense of control and security.

Sacralising the Profane: Rites and rituals allowed for the sacralisation of everyday life and ordinary objects. By designating certain spaces, objects, or actions as sacred, early humans sought to imbue them with a higher significance and connect them to the divine or supernatural realm.

Over time, as human societies evolved and developed more complex belief systems, the range and intricacy of rites and rituals expanded. Religious institutions, priesthoods, and specialized roles and functions emerged to administer and oversee these practices. As cultures interacted and exchanged ideas, rituals also underwent changes, adaptations, and syncretism, incorporating elements from different traditions. Additionally, rites and rituals evolved to address the changing needs and concerns of communities. They encompassed a wide range of purposes, including supplication for good fortune, fertility rites, initiation ceremonies, healing rituals, harvest celebrations, and commemorations of important events or historical figures.

It is important to note that the specific forms of worship, rites, and rituals vary greatly across different cultures, religions, and historical periods. They are influenced by geographical, historical, social, and cultural factors, resulting in a rich tapestry of diverse practices and beliefs around the world. The first forms of worship likely emerged as early humans sought to connect with and understand the forces they perceived as divine or supernatural. Rites and rituals became integral to the worship process due to their ability to establish communication, convey symbolism, foster social cohesion, provide order, and sacralise the ordinary. As societies evolved and belief systems developed, rites and rituals expanded in complexity and diversity, adapting to the changing needs and contexts of human communities

The philosophy of the sacred and profane plays a significant role in the context of Goddess worship, as it helps delineate the realms of the divine and the mundane, and highlights the transformative power of connecting with the sacred. The terms "sacred" and "profane" were introduced by French sociologist Émile Durkheim in his seminal work "The Elementary Forms of Religious Life." According to Durkheim, the sacred refers to the realm of the extraordinary, the transcendent, and the divine, while the profane pertains to the everyday, mundane, and secular aspects of life. These concepts are not necessarily dichotomous, but rather represent distinct categories of experience and perception.

In the context of Goddess worship, the sacred is intimately connected with the divine feminine and the qualities she embodies, such as love, wisdom, nurturing, and creative power. The Goddess represents the transcendent aspect of the sacred, inspiring awe, reverence, and a sense of the numinous. Through her various forms and attributes, she serves as a channel to access deeper levels of consciousness and spiritual insight.

Goddess worship often involves creating sacred spaces, such as temples, altars, or natural settings, where devotees can engage in rituals, meditation, or contemplation. These spaces are imbued with a heightened sense of the sacred, and through their sanctification, they provide a tangible connection to the divine presence. The practice of Goddess worship invites individuals to transcend the limitations of mundane existence and enter into a sacred relationship with the divine. It offers a pathway to experience the numinous and to tap into the transformative power of the Goddess. By engaging in devotional practices, such as prayers, chants, or offerings, individuals seek to establish a connection with the sacred realm and align themselves with the divine energies.

One of the key aspects of Goddess worship is the recognition of the inherent sacredness in all aspects of life, including the profane. The Goddess is not confined to an isolated realm separate from the world, but rather permeates every aspect of existence. This perspective calls for a holistic understanding that the sacred can be found in nature, in human relationships, in daily activities, and in the self.

By acknowledging the sacred within the profane, Goddess worship encourages individuals to cultivate a mindful and reverential approach to life. It invites a shift in perception, where the ordinary becomes infused with the extraordinary, and the mundane becomes a source of inspiration and spiritual growth. The Goddess, in her many forms, offers guidance and support in navigating the complexities of everyday life, infusing it with meaning, purpose, and a sense of sacredness.

The philosophy of the sacred and profane within Goddess worship also carries implications for personal transformation and empowerment. The Goddess is often associated with qualities such as strength, courage, and liberation. By connecting with her energy, individuals can tap into their own innate power and potential, transcending limiting beliefs and societal constraints. This process involves recognizing and embracing the sacred aspects of their own being and cultivating a deep sense of self-worth and authenticity.

Furthermore, Goddess worship challenges traditional patriarchal notions that have often marginalized and suppressed the feminine. By celebrating the divine feminine, the philosophy of the sacred and profane supports gender equality, inclusivity, and the reclamation of women's power and agency. It serves as a counterbalance to the patriarchal dominance that has often characterized religious and social structures, offering a vision of harmony and balance between the masculine and feminine energies.

The philosophy of the sacred and profane in the context of Goddess worship provides a framework for understanding the interplay between the transcendent and the mundane. It emphasizes the importance of recognizing and cultivating the sacred in all aspects of life, while also honouring the divine feminine and embracing personal transformation. Through Goddess worship, individuals can embark on a spiritual journey that transcends the limitations of everyday existence, connecting with the sacred and harnessing its transformative power for personal growth, empowerment, and the creation of a more balanced and harmonious world.

Belief in the Goddess can indeed be seen as a form of psychotherapy for some individuals, as it provides emotional support, a sense of security, and psychological well-being. Belief in the Goddess can function as a form of psychotherapy and can provide security to believers.

Emotional Support: Belief in the Goddess offers emotional support to believers by providing a comforting and nurturing presence. The Goddess is often associated with qualities such as compassion, love, and understanding. Devotees find solace in the belief that the Goddess is there to listen, support, and guide them through life's challenges. This emotional connection can offer a sense of validation, reassurance, and comfort during times of distress or uncertainty.

Symbolic Representation: The Goddess serves as a symbolic representation of the divine feminine and its empowering qualities. This symbolism can help individuals tap into their own inner resources and strengths. By identifying with the

Goddess and her attributes, believers can gain a sense of empowerment, resilience, and self-confidence. This can be particularly beneficial for individuals seeking to overcome self-doubt, trauma, or feelings of powerlessness.

Psychological Integration: The belief in the Goddess can aid in psychological integration by embracing the full spectrum of human experiences and emotions. The Goddess encompasses various archetypes and aspects, representing the light and shadow aspects of existence. Through the worship and exploration of different Goddess forms, individuals can engage in a process of self-reflection, self-acceptance, and integration of their own complex emotions and experiences.

Rituals and Practices: Engaging in rituals and practices associated with Goddess worship can have therapeutic benefits. Rituals provide structure, a sense of continuity, and a feeling of control in an unpredictable world. They offer a space for self-expression, release of emotions, and connection with the divine. Rituals can serve as a form of catharsis, promoting healing, emotional well-being, and a sense of belonging to a supportive community.

Empowerment and Agency: Belief in the Goddess often promotes a sense of personal empowerment and agency. The Goddess is often depicted as a strong, independent, and assertive figure. By identifying with the Goddess, believers can tap into their own innate power, develop a sense of self-worth, and actively shape their lives. This empowerment can enhance self-esteem, foster a proactive mind-set, and promote a sense of control over one's circumstances.

Community and Belonging: Goddess worship often takes place within a community or supportive group. Believers can find a sense of belonging, connection, and mutual support among like-minded individuals. This communal aspect of Goddess worship provides a social support network, opportunities for shared rituals, and a sense of collective identity. Belonging to a community that shares similar beliefs and values can contribute to a feeling of security and belonging.

The earliest texts that mention Goddess worship in India can be found in the ancient scriptures known as the Vedas. The Vedas are a collection of sacred texts composed in Sanskrit between 1500 and 500 BCE. They form the foundation of Hinduism and contain hymns, rituals, and philosophical teachings. Within the Vedas, there are several hymns dedicated to various goddesses, indicating the presence and significance of Goddess worship in ancient India. The Rigveda, the oldest of the four Vedas, contains hymns that venerate goddesses such as Ushas, Aditi, and Saraswati. Here are some specific references:

Rigveda: In the Rigveda, there are hymns dedicated to Ushas, the goddess of dawn. For example, in Rigveda 1.48, a hymn praises Ushas and her radiant beauty, portraying her as a divine and life-giving force.

Rigveda: Hymn 10.125 of the Rigveda is known as the "Devi Sukta" or the "Hymn to the Goddess." It is a significant hymn that celebrates the feminine divine in various forms. It praises the Goddess as the ultimate source of creation, power, and wisdom.

Rigveda: Aditi, the mother goddess, is mentioned in several hymns in the Rigveda. Hymn 1.89 praises Aditi as the great cosmic mother and the protector of all beings.

Atharvaveda: The Atharvaveda, another Vedic text, also contains hymns dedicated to goddesses. One notable hymn is in Atharvaveda 12.1, which praises the goddess Earth (Prithvi) as a nurturing and benevolent deity.

These references demonstrate that the worship of goddesses was present in the earliest Vedic literature. While these texts don't provide a comprehensive understanding of Goddess worship, they establish a foundation for the subsequent development of Goddess-centric traditions and rituals in India.

It is important to note that the Vedas contain complex and symbolic language, and interpretations of these hymns can vary. The understanding of goddesses and their roles evolved over time through subsequent scriptures, epics, and regional traditions that expanded on the Vedic foundations.

Inscriptions of Goddesses on Coins:

Ancient coins with inscriptions of Goddesses provide valuable evidence of the emergence and prevalence of Goddess worship in various regions. These coins, minted during different periods of ancient history, feature depictions and inscriptions related to different goddesses, often reflecting the religious and cultural practices of the time.

Highlighting few notable examples:

Coinage of the Kushan Empire: The Kushan Empire, which existed from the 1st to the 3rd century CE in the Indian subcontinent, Central Asia, and parts of present-day Iran, produced coins featuring various deities, including goddesses. Coins of the Kushan ruler Kanishka depict the goddess Ardoxsho (Greek: Artemis), who was worshipped in both Greek and Zoroastrian traditions.

Coins of the Western Kshatrapas: The Western Kshatrapas were a dynasty that ruled western India from the 1st to the 4th century CE. Some of their coins depict goddesses such as Ardoksho (Artemis), Bhagavati (a generic term for goddess), and Nana (a regional goddess associated with fertility).

Coins of the Gupta Empire: The Gupta Empire, which flourished from the 4th to the 6th century CE in northern India, produced coins featuring goddesses. Some Gupta coins depict Lakshmi, the goddess of wealth and prosperity, seated on a lotus.

Coins of the Chalukyas: The Chalukya dynasty, which ruled parts of southern and western India from the 6th to the 12th century CE, minted coins featuring goddesses. Coins of the Badami Chalukyas, for instance, bear the image of the goddess Durga standing or seated on a lion.

Coins of the Cholas: The Chola dynasty, which ruled parts of southern India from the 9th to the 13th century CE, issued coins featuring goddesses. Some Chola coins depict the goddess Lakshmi and the regional deity Bhuvaneswari.

Coins of the Vijayanagara Empire: The Vijayanagara Empire, which thrived from the 14th to the 17th century CE in southern India, minted coins featuring various deities, including goddesses. Coins of the Vijayanagara rulers depict goddesses such as Lakshmi and Bhuvaneswari.

These examples illustrate the presence of goddesses and Goddess worship in the iconography and inscriptions of ancient coins. The depiction of goddesses on these coins suggests the importance of female deities in religious and cultural practices of the time. It provides evidence of the recognition and veneration of goddesses in the societies that produced these coins, indicating the emergence and prevalence of Goddess worship in those regions during ancient times.

In ancient Buddhism, there were several prominent goddess figures who were revered and worshipped in Buddhist shrines and stupas. These goddesses were venerated long before the emergence of the goddesses of the Hindu pantheon. Here are some notable ancient Buddhist goddesses:

Hariti: Hariti was a popular goddess in ancient Buddhist traditions, particularly in the Mahayana and Vajrayana schools. Originally depicted as a female demon who caused the death of children, she underwent a transformation and became a benevolent protector of children. Hariti is often depicted with multiple arms, holding children in her arms or surrounded by them. Shrines dedicated to Hariti were established, and she was worshipped for the well-being and protection of children.

Tara: Tara is one of the most significant and widely revered goddesses in Buddhism. She is believed to have originated as a feminine aspect of the bodhisattva Avalokiteshvara. Tara is associated with compassion, protection, and liberation. She is often depicted as a green or white deity with multiple arms, representing her ability to swiftly respond to the needs of sentient beings. Various forms of Tara, such as Green Tara and White Tara, are worshipped in Buddhist shrines and temples across different Buddhist traditions.

Prajnaparamita: Prajnaparamita is not a specific goddess but rather the personification of the perfection of wisdom, an essential concept in Mahayana Buddhism. Prajnaparamita is revered as the embodiment of transcendent wisdom and enlightenment. In visual representations, Prajnaparamita is depicted as a female deity, often seated on a lotus throne and holding a book or a lotus. She is associated with profound insight, clarity, and the realization of ultimate truth.

Vasudhara: Vasudhara is a goddess associated with wealth, abundance, and prosperity. She is worshipped in both Hinduism and Buddhism, and her prominence in Buddhist traditions predates the emergence of Hindu goddesses. Vasudhara is often depicted with multiple arms, holding various symbolic attributes such as a sheaf of grain, a treasure vase, and a lotus. Devotees pray to Vasudhara for material wealth, spiritual abundance, and the removal of obstacles.

These ancient Buddhist goddesses were revered and worshipped in Buddhist shrines and stupas long before the development of the elaborate pantheon of Hindu goddesses. They played significant roles in the religious and spiritual practices of ancient Buddhist communities, offering devotees protection, blessings, and guidance on their path towards enlightenment. The presence of these goddess figures within Buddhism reflects the recognition and reverence of feminine divine qualities and the incorporation of goddess worship within Buddhist traditions.

Stone Age Goddesses:

During the Stone Age, which spans a vast period of prehistoric human history, worship and reverence for deities played a significant role in the lives of early human communities. While archaeological evidence from this era is limited, there are indications that the Stone Age societies practiced a form of religious belief, often centered around female deities or goddesses. These ancient goddesses were associated with various aspects of nature, fertility, and the cycles of life. While specific details and names of these goddesses are mostly speculative, we can draw upon archaeological findings and anthropological research to gain some insight into the worship of Stone Age goddesses.

The Mother Goddess: One of the prominent goddess archetypes during the Stone Age is the Mother Goddess. She represents the life-giving and nurturing qualities associated with fertility and childbirth. Artifacts such as the Venus figurines, found across Europe and dating back to the Upper Paleolithic period, are believed to symbolize the worship of the Mother Goddess. These figurines depict women with exaggerated sexual characteristics, emphasizing the importance of fertility and the continuation of the human race.

Earth Goddess: The worship of the Earth Goddess, also known as the Great Goddess, was prevalent during the Stone Age. This goddess personified the Earth itself and was revered as the giver of life and sustenance. She was associated with the fertility of the land, agriculture, and the abundance of resources necessary for survival. The worship of the Earth Goddess reflected the Stone Age communities' reliance on nature for sustenance and their deep connection with the environment.

Lunar Goddess: The cycles of the moon held great significance for early human societies, and thus the worship of a Lunar Goddess was widespread during the Stone Age. The lunar cycle was often associated with fertility, menstruation, and the tides. The goddess embodied the changing phases of the moon and the interconnectedness between nature and human existence. The Lunar Goddess represented the feminine divine power associated with transformation, renewal, and intuition.

Huntress Goddess: In hunter-gatherer societies, the successful pursuit of game was crucial for survival. Consequently, a Huntress Goddess was venerated during the Stone Age. This goddess embodied strength, agility, and hunting prowess. She provided guidance and protection for hunters and was revered as the guardian of animal populations. Examples of cave paintings and rock art, such as the cave of Lascaux in France, depict hunting scenes and suggest the existence of a goddess associated with the hunt.

Ancestor Goddess: Stone Age communities recognized the importance of their ancestors and the continuity of generations. An Ancestor Goddess was worshipped, representing the spirits of the departed and the wisdom of previous generations. She provided guidance, protection, and blessings to the living. Rituals honoring ancestors, including burial practices and the creation of ancestral altars, suggest the veneration of an Ancestor Goddess.

It is essential to note that the information about Stone Age goddesses is limited and subject to interpretation. Much of our understanding is derived from artifacts, cave paintings, and anthropological research. The specific names and characteristics of these goddesses remain speculative, but the themes and roles align with the cultural practices and beliefs prevalent during the Stone Age.

Chapter 2

Evolution of the Goddess

The pre-historic man worshipped different elements of nature for fear of their potential to inflict calamities or curse as well as in reverence for the benefits he received from them. His sense of gratitude went to the extent of bestowing godhood of such forces of nature as the sun, rain, river, forest, mountain, animal and plants etc. Gradually, temples and other religious institutions were created and elaborate rituals as well as functions were performed there to appease the presiding deities. He offered them specific materials of his choice including leaf, flower, fruit, seeds etc. and also used different plant products in those religious activities. The temple has always been regarded as a sacred place in Hinduism. "Sacred" is derived from the Latin root sacrare (http://www.merriam-webster.com/dictionary/sacred), which means to dedicate exclusively for the service of the gods. A "sanctum" is a place of inviolable privacy. On the other hand, "profane", derived from the Latin profanus, is that which relates to the uninitiated or ordinary life. (http://www.merriam-webster.com/dictionary/sacred)

The institutions of temples and their traditions play a vital role in the socio-cultural landscapes of many societies today. The "sacredness" in Hindu temples is interpreted from several aspects - with respect to physical attributes and spatial arrangements, which channelize the focus of devotees on the sacredness contained within the temple, in contrast to the "profaneness" of the surrounding world. Divinity is a concept much emphasized in Hinduism and other world religions. The word 'divine', over time has been associated with God and supernatural powers. Ancient Indian texts elaborate about divinities with regard to the many Gods of the Hindu pantheon. They, in turn have influenced the myths of later times and modern religions. Despite several million gods that are venerated in Hinduism, the high priests and mendicants understand and believe in the existence of One Supreme God – Brahman.

The "Divine Feminine" and its interpretations has been considered significant in many cultures and traditions. Cultural traditions around the world indicate the presence of goddess worship together with the reverence accorded to the role of the female in life and reproductive cycle. Trans-human reality has also been incorporated in non-theistic Buddhism in connection with Vajrayana Buddhism. This transcends the human experiences and is complex yet subtle, sourced from Indian textual and artistic relics (Shaw, p 4). In addition to the enlightened female forms of Buddha, Shaw also pointed out there are twenty-two goddesses in the historical phases of Indian Buddhism.

A goddess is a female deity. In many known cultures, goddesses are often linked with literal or metaphorical pregnancy or imagined feminine roles associated with how women and girls are perceived or expected to behave. This includes themes of spinning, weaving, beauty, love, sexuality, motherhood, domesticity, creativity, and fertility (exemplified by the ancient mother goddess cult). Many major goddesses are also associated with magic, war, strategy, hunting, farming, wisdom, fate, earth, sky, power, laws, justice, and more. Some themes, such as discord or disease, which are considered negative within their cultural contexts also are found associated with some goddesses. There are as many differently described and understood goddesses as there are male, shapeshifting, or neuter gods. In some faiths, a sacred female figure holds a central place in religious prayer and worship. For example, Shaktism, the worship of the female force that animates the world, is one of the three major sects of Hinduism. Polytheist religions honour multiple goddesses and gods, and usually view them as discrete, separate beings. These deities may be part of a pantheon, or different regions may have tutelary deities.

Ancient Near East

Mesopotamia

Inanna was the most worshipped goddess in ancient Sumer. She was later syncretised with the East Semitic goddess Ishtar. Other Mesopotamian goddesses include Ninhursag, Ninlil, Antu and Gaga.

Ancient Africa (Egypt)

Goddesses of the Ennead of Heliopolis: Tefnut, Nut, Nephthys, Isis

Goddesses of the Ogdoad of Hermopolis: Naunet, Amaunet, Kauket, Hauhet; originally a cult of Hathor

Satis and Anuket of the triad of Elephantine

Canaan

Goddesses of the Canaanite religion: Ba`alat Gebal, Astarte, Anat.

Anatolia

Cybele: Her Hittite name was Kubaba, but her name changed to Cybele in Phrygian and Roman culture. Her effect can be also seen on Artemis as the Lady of Ephesus.

Hebat: Mother Goddess of the Hittite pantheon and wife of the leader sky god, Teshub. She was the origin of the Hurrian cult.

Arinniti: Hittite Goddess of the sun. She became patron of the Hittite Empire and monarchy.

Leto: A mother Goddess figure in Lykia. She was also the main goddess of the capital city of Lykia League (Letoon)

Pre-Islamic Arabia

In pre-Islamic Mecca the goddesses Uzza, Manāt and al-Lāt were known as "the daughters of god". Uzzā was worshipped by the Nabataeans, who equated her with the Graeco-Roman goddesses Aphrodite, Urania, Venus and Caelestis. Each of the three goddesses had a separate shrine near Mecca. Uzzā, was called upon for protection by the pre-Islamic Quraysh. "In 624 at the battle called "Uhud", the war cry of the Qurayshites was, "O people of Uzzā, people of Hubal!" (Tawil 1993).

According to Ibn Ishaq's controversial account of the Satanic Verses (q.v.), these verses had previously endorsed them as intercessors for Muslims, but were abrogated. Most Muslim scholars have regarded the story as historically implausible, while opinion is divided among western scholars such as Leone Caetani and John Burton, who argue against, and William Muir and William Montgomery Watt, who argue for its plausibility.

Indo-European traditions

Pre-Christian and pre-Islamic goddesses in cultures that spoke Indo-European languages.

Indian

Proto-Indo-Iranian religion and Rigvedic deities

Ushas: is the main goddess of the Rigveda and is the goddess of the dawn.

Prithivi: the Earth, also appears as a goddess. Rivers are also deified as goddesses.

Agneya: or Aagneya is the Hindu Goddess of Fire.

Varuni: is the Hindu Goddess of Water. Bhumi, Janani, Buvana, and Prithvi are names of the Hindu Goddess of Earth.

Iranian

Anahita: or Anahit, or Nahid, or Arədvī Sūrā Anāhitā, or Aban: the divinity of "the Waters" and hence associated with fertility, healing, beauty and wisdom.

Daena: a divinity, counted among the yazatas, representing insight and revelation, hence "conscience" or "religion".

Spenta Armaiti: or Sandaramet, one of the Amesha Spentas, a female divinity associated with earth and Mother Nature. She is also associated with the female virtue of devotion (to family, husband, and child). In the Iranian calendar, her name is on the twelfth month and also the fifth day of the month.

Ashi: a divinity of fertility and fortune in the Zoroastrian hierarchy of yazatas.

Greco-Roman

Portrait-Statue of an unknown woman as Ceres, Roman goddess of agriculture and motherly relationships

Eleusinian Mysteries: Baubo (goddess of mirth), Demeter (goddess of the harvest) and Persephone (goddess of spring, queen of the Underworld as the wife of Hades).

Greek muses: Calliope (goddess of epic poetry), Clio (history), Erato (love poetry), Euterpe (music, song, and lyric poetry), Melpomene (tragedy), Polyhymnia (sacred poetry), Terpsichore (dance), Thalia (comedy and pastoral poetry), and Urania (astronomy).

Aphrodite: Goddess of love and beauty.

Artemis: Virgin goddess of the wilderness and the hunt.

Athena: Virgin goddess of strategy, warfare, and crafts.

Eris: Goddess of chaos.

Gaia: Primordial goddess of the Earth. Most gods descend from her.

Hecate: Goddess of sorcery and crossroads. Often considered a chthonic or lunar goddess. She is either portrayed as a single goddess or a triple goddess (maiden, mother, crone).

Hera: Goddess of womanhood, marriage and childbirth, queen of Olympus as the wife of Zeus.

Hestia: Virgin goddess of the hearth, domesticity and family.

Iris: Goddess of rainbows.

Leto: Titan goddess of childhood.

Nike: Goddess of victory. She is predominantly pictured

with Zeus or Athena and sometimes Ares.

Selene: Titan goddess of the Moon.

Rhea: Titan goddess of motherhood.

Celtic

Main article: Celtic pantheon

Goddesses and Otherworldly Women in Celtic polytheism include:

Celtic antiquity: Brigantia

Gallo-Roman goddesses: Epona, Dea Matrona

Irish mythology: Áine, Boann, Brigid, The Cailleach, Danu, Ériu, Fand and The Morrígan (Nemain, Macha, and Badb) among others.

The Celts honoured goddesses of nature and natural forces, as well as those connected with skills and professions such as healing, warfare and poetry. The Celtic goddesses have diverse qualities such as abundance, creation and beauty, as well as harshness, slaughter and vengeance. They have been depicted as beautiful or hideous, old hags or young women, and at times may transform their appearance from one state to another, or into their associated creatures such as crows, cows, wolves or eels, to name but a few. In Irish mythology in particular, tutelary goddesses are often associated with sovereignty and various features of the land, notably mountains, rivers, forests and holy wells.

Pre-Columbian America

Aztec

Xochiquetzal (left) and Chalchiuhtlicue (right) as depicted in the Tovar Codex.

Chalchiuhtlicue: goddess of water (rivers, seas, storms, etc.)

Chantico: goddess of the hearth, flames

Coyolxauhqui: warrior goddess associated with the moon

Duality Earth Goddesses: Cihuacoatl (childbirth and maternal death), Coatlicue (earth as the womb and grave), Tlazolteotl (filth and purification)

Itzpapalotl: monstrous ruler of Tamoanchan (a paradise realm)

Mictecacihuatl: queen of Mictlan (the underworld)

Xochiquetzal: goddess of fertility, beauty, and female sexuality

Maya

Ixchel: mother goddess

Maya moon goddess

Goddess I: eroticism, human procreation, and marriage

Inca

Pachamama: the supreme Mother Earth

Mama Killa: moon goddess

Mama Ocllo: fertility goddess

Mama Cocha: goddess of the sea and lakes

Native North America

Goddesses of various Native North American peoples include:

Spider Grandmother: Creator goddess of the Southwestern United States

Atahensic: Iroquois sky goddess

Atira: Pawnee earth and corn goddess

Tia: Haida goddess of peaceful death

Sedna: Inuit goddess of the sea and underworld

Atabey: Taino mother goddess

(https://en.wikipedia.org/wiki/Goddess)

Hinduism

Devi, the Divine Female, revered by all, is universally known as the Mother Goddess. Devi, the Goddess, regarded as mother and is now since ages the Mother Goddess. The Mother Goddess is India's supreme Divinity. Myriad are her shrines and unending her boons. Centuries long tradition of worship has woven around her innumerable myths and the devotional mind has discovered in her oceans of mercy. In fury or in frown, she is always the same protective, caring, loving Mother with a benign face and a blessing hand. (Jain & Daljeet)

The worship of goddesses, often referred to as "Goddess worship" or "the cult of the goddess," has a rich and complex history that spans across cultures and continents. This form of religious devotion has evolved over millennia, with significant variations in beliefs and practices.

Global Evolution of Goddess Worship:

Palaeolithic and Neolithic Periods:

The roots of goddess worship can be traced back to the Palaeolithic and Neolithic periods when early human societies relied heavily on agriculture and recognized the cyclical patterns of nature. Female figurines and fertility symbols found at archaeological sites suggest the reverence of a mother goddess associated with fertility and abundance.

Ancient Mesopotamia:

In ancient Mesopotamia, around 3500 BCE, goddesses like Inanna and Ishtar were worshipped as powerful deities embodying both love and war. They played pivotal roles in the pantheon of gods and were associated with aspects of human life and nature.

Ancient Egypt:

Egypt had a pantheon of goddesses, with Isis being one of the most prominent. She represented magic, fertility, and motherhood and was revered by both commoners and royalty. The concept of the divine feminine was integral to Egyptian religion.

Greco-Roman Civilization:

In ancient Greece and Rome, goddesses like Athena, Aphrodite, and Artemis held significant positions in the pantheon. Each goddess had distinct attributes and was worshipped for her specific domain, such as wisdom, love, or hunting.

Celtic and Norse Cultures:

In Celtic and Norse cultures, goddesses like Brigid and Freyja were venerated for their roles in the natural world, including agriculture, healing, and fertility.

Indigenous and Native Cultures:

Many indigenous and Native American cultures across the Americas also have traditions of goddess worship. These traditions are often deeply connected to the land, nature, and the balance of life.

Goddess Worship in India:

India has a long and multifaceted history of goddess worship, often referred to as "Shakti" or "Devi" worship.

Key phases of its evolution:

Indus Valley Civilization (c. 3300–1300 BCE):

The Indus Valley Civilization, one of the world's oldest urban civilizations, provides evidence of goddess worship through various female figurines and seals. Scholars believe these artefacts represent a mother goddess or fertility goddess.

Vedic Period (c. 1500–500 BCE):

In the early Vedic texts, there is a reverence for various female deities, such as Ushas (the goddess of dawn) and Prithvi (the earth goddess). However, the emphasis was on male deities during this period.

Puranic Period (c. 300 BCE–500 CE):

The worship of goddesses gained prominence during the Puranic period with the emergence of texts like the Devi Mahatmya (part of the Markandeya Purana) that extol the power and significance of the divine feminine, particularly in the form of Goddess Durga.

Tantric Traditions (c. 6th century CE onward):

Tantric practices in Hinduism gave rise to an array of goddess forms, each representing different aspects of the divine feminine energy (Shakti). This period saw the rise of goddesses like Kali, Tara, and Tripura Sundari.

Bhakti and Devotional Movements:

In various regions of India, Bhakti and devotional movements further popularized goddess worship. For example, the worship of Goddess Lakshmi, Saraswati, and Durga became integral to Hindu devotional practices.

Modern Goddess Worship:

In contemporary India, goddess worship continues to be a vibrant aspect of Hinduism and other regional religions. Festivals like Navratri and Durga Puja celebrate the divine feminine, and temples dedicated to goddesses are widespread.

The evolution and history of goddess worship is deeply intertwined with the development of human civilizations and their understanding of nature, fertility, and the divine. This practice has evolved differently across cultures and regions but remains a significant and enduring aspect of many spiritual traditions worldwide, including in India.

The book focusses on lesser known Goddesses or those forgotten over time. The phenomenon of gods and goddesses being forgotten over time and fading into the past can be attributed to several interconnected factors:

Cultural Change and Evolution: Cultures and societies evolve over time. As they do, belief systems, values, and religious practices often change as well. The deities worshipped by one generation may not hold the same significance or relevance for future generations. Cultural shifts can lead to the decline or abandonment of certain gods and goddesses.

Religious Syncretism: Over centuries, different cultures and religions often interact and influence each other. This can lead to the merging or syncretism of religious beliefs. In this process, certain gods and goddesses may lose their distinct identities as they are incorporated into a broader religious framework or replaced by deities from other traditions.

Political and Social Changes: Political and social upheavals can also influence religious practices. When societies undergo significant transformations, rulers and elites may promote or discourage particular religious beliefs and practices. This can result in the decline of certain deities if they fall out of favor with those in power.

Loss of Written Records: In many cases, the historical record of ancient religions is limited, and written records can be lost or destroyed over time. Without written documentation, it becomes challenging to preserve and pass down knowledge of specific gods and goddesses to future generations.

Shift in Worldview: As societies advance technologically and scientifically, there may be a shift in the way people view the world. Some individuals may become less inclined to believe in supernatural beings or may adopt more secular worldviews, leading to a decline in religious practices and the relevance of gods and goddesses.

Cultural Amnesia: As societies modernize and become more cosmopolitan, there can be a loss of cultural memory. Younger generations may not be as connected to their cultural and religious heritage, leading to the fading of belief in and knowledge of ancient deities.

Natural Disasters and Catastrophes: Historical events such as natural disasters, wars, and epidemics can disrupt religious practices and result in the abandonment of certain deities. These events may be interpreted as divine punishment or may lead to a re-evaluation of religious beliefs.

Religious Reform and Revival Movements: Sometimes, religious reform movements within a tradition seek to return to the roots of the faith and purify it by eliminating certain gods or practices considered impure or heretical. These movements can contribute to the decline of certain deities.

Globalization: In today's interconnected world, exposure to a wide range of religious beliefs and practices can lead to the adoption of new religious traditions or the dilution of indigenous belief systems. As a result, local gods and goddesses may be overshadowed by more dominant or globalized faiths.

Overall, the fading of gods and goddesses over time is a complex process influenced by cultural, social, political, and historical factors. While some deities may be forgotten, others may continue to evolve and adapt to changing times, and some may even experience revival in response to cultural or spiritual movements.

The phenomenon of forgotten goddesses is prevalent across different cultures and historical periods. Some goddesses who have been largely forgotten or are no longer actively remembered and worshipped are:

1. Ananke (Greece): Ananke was the ancient Greek

goddess of necessity and inevitability. She represented the primordial force that governed fate and destiny. While she played a significant role in early Greek cosmology, her worship waned over time as the focus shifted to other gods and goddesses in the Greek pantheon.

2. Anat (Mesopotamia): Anat was a prominent goddess in ancient Mesopotamian and Canaanite cultures, associated with war and fertility. As these civilizations evolved and were replaced by others, Anat's worship diminished, and she became a less central figure in the religious beliefs of the region.

3. Nehalennia (Roman Empire): Nehalennia was a goddess worshipped in the Roman Empire, particularly in the coastal regions of what is now the Netherlands and Belgium. She was associated with seafaring, trade, and protection. With the decline of the Roman Empire and the spread of Christianity, Nehalennia's cult faded into obscurity.

4. Mawu-Lisa (West Africa): Mawu-Lisa is a dual-gendered deity worshipped by the Fon and Ewe peoples of West Africa. Mawu represents the moon, fertility, and life, while Lisa represents the sun, death, and the sky. While still revered by some practitioners of traditional African religions, Mawu-Lisa's worship has declined in many areas due to the influence of Christianity and Islam.

5. Seshat (Ancient Egypt): Seshat was the ancient Egyptian goddess of wisdom, writing, and measurement. She was associated with record-keeping and architectural planning. As Egyptian society changed and other deities like Thoth and Isis gained prominence, Seshat's significance dwindled.

6. Xochiquetzal (Aztec Empire): Xochiquetzal was the Aztec goddess of beauty, love, and fertility. With the Spanish conquest and the suppression of indigenous religions, the worship of Xochiquetzal and other Aztec deities was forcibly replaced by Christianity, resulting in their decline and near-forgotten status.

7. Astarte (Phoenicia and Levant): Astarte was a widely worshipped goddess in Phoenician and Levantine cultures, associated with love, fertility, and war. As these cultures were assimilated into larger empires and as new religious traditions emerged, Astarte's veneration diminished.

8. Epona (Celtic and Roman Cultures): Epona was a Celtic goddess associated with horses and fertility. Her worship spread across Celtic regions and into the Roman Empire. However, with the decline of Celtic civilization and the rise of Christianity, Epona's cult gradually faded away.

9. Camaxtli (Aztec Empire): Camaxtli was the Aztec god of hunting, war, and fate. His worship declined significantly following the Spanish conquest and the suppression of Aztec religion. The memory of Camaxtli largely faded from mainstream consciousness.

10. Hathor-Tefnut (Ancient Egypt): Hathor-Tefnut was a dual-goddess in ancient Egyptian mythology, representing aspects of music, dance, and moisture. Over time, her worship became less prominent as the focus shifted to other Egyptian deities like Osiris, Isis, and Ra.

These examples illustrate how various goddesses from different cultures and time periods have been forgotten or lost relevance due to historical, cultural, and religious changes. While some may still exist in mythologies and historical records, their worship and active recognition have significantly diminished or disappeared as societies evolved and religious beliefs shifted.

The Hindu tradition is rich and diverse, with a vast pantheon of deities, including numerous goddesses who have played significant roles in mythology, religious rituals, and cultural practices. However, like in many other religious traditions, there are also goddesses within Hinduism who have been forgotten or have lost prominence over time. Here are a few examples:

1. **Chhaya:** Chhaya, whose name means "shadow" or "shade," was a lesser-known goddess in Hindu mythology. She was the second wife of Lord Surya (the Sun god) and was often associated with patience and self-sacrifice. While not completely forgotten, her role and worship have diminished in comparison to other solar deities like Surya and Savitri.

2. **Jyestha:** Jyestha, sometimes referred to as Jyestha Devi, is the elder sister of Goddess Lakshmi, the goddess of wealth and prosperity. Jyestha is associated with misfortune and is sometimes considered inauspicious. Her worship is not as common as that of her younger sister Lakshmi, who embodies good fortune.

3. **Varuni:** Varuni is the goddess of wine and intoxication in Hindu mythology. She is often associated with the Varuni beverage mentioned in ancient texts. While Varuni's existence is acknowledged in some scriptures, her worship and significance have largely faded, likely due to the social and religious implications of alcohol consumption in Hinduism.

4. **Bhuvaneswari:** Bhuvaneswari is a goddess who represents the material world and the universe. Her name means "Queen of the Universe." While

she is recognized in some sects of Hinduism, her worship is not as widespread or well-known as that of goddesses like Durga, Kali, or Saraswati.

5. **Katyayani:** Katyayani is one of the forms of Goddess Durga and is revered primarily during the Navratri festival. While she is well-known during this period, her worship is relatively limited compared to other forms of Durga, such as Mahakali or Mahalakshmi.

6. **Jayanti:** Jayanti is a goddess who is sometimes mentioned in Hindu scriptures as the daughter of Indra, the king of the gods. Her role and worship are not as prominent as other goddesses like Saraswati or Parvati, who have more elaborate mythologies.

7. **Vasavi Kanyaka Parameshwari:** Vasavi Kanyaka Parameshwari is a regional goddess primarily worshipped in parts of South India. Her worship is not as widespread as some of the more prominent Hindu goddesses, and she is often associated with specific local traditions.

It's important to note that the forgotten goddesses in Hinduism may still have pockets of dedicated worshipers and may be part of regional or local traditions. Additionally, the prominence of specific deities can vary widely across different sects and regions within Hinduism. The tradition's vast and diverse nature allows for a wide range of beliefs and practices, and while some goddesses may have faded from the mainstream, they can still hold significance for certain communities and individuals within the Hindu faith.

Chapter 3

Forgotten Goddesses

Ganga

Elaborated in the Mahabharata as the 'best of rivers, born of all the sacred waters', the Ganges is personified as the goddess Ganga. Ganga's mother is Mena and her father

is Himavat, the personification of the Himalaya mountains. In a myth Ganga marries King Sanatanu but the bond comes to a tragic end when the goddess is discovered to have drowned her own children. In the Mahabharata, Ganga is the mother of Bhishma and in some myths Skanda (Karttikeya), the Hindu god of war, is her son with Agni, the god of fire.

The Ganges appears in Hindu mythology often as a background location, for example, as a place where the famous figures Atri performed various acts of asceticism. In the Siva Purana, the Ganges carries the seed of Shiva which, when carried to a clump of reeds, became Skanda. In the Matsya Purana and the story of the Great Flood the first man Manu throws a giant fish into the river which then continues to grow to gigantic proportions, eventually escaping to the sea.

Mythology associated with Ganga apart, we cannot ignore its importance. The river is the source of life of the people. Despite being a symbol of the sacred, it is polluted in an unbelievable manner.

Sun Goddess Amaterasu

Amaterasu, goddess of the Shinto religion is considered primarily a sun goddess and ruler of the Takama no Hara (the High Celestial Plain), the realm of the kami or spirits. She is also identified as the key ancestor for all Emperors of Japan.

She is more than just the shining sun: she is a loving goddess who provides for people and protects them. Amaterasu was the first to cultivate rice in heaven. She also invented and taught people the arts of weaving and cultivating silkworms. Rice, silk, fabric: all are gifts of Amaterasu (and are offerings to bestow upon her).

Amaterasu's chief place of worship is the Grand Shrine of Ise, the foremost Shintō shrine in Japan. She is

manifested there in a mirror that is one of the three Imperial Treasures of Japan (the other two being a jewelled necklace and a sword). The genders of Amaterasu and her brother the moon god Tsukiyomi no Mikato are remarkable exceptions in worldwide mythology of the sun and the moon.

Ishtar

Mesopotamian goddess

Ishtar, (Sumerian Inanna) in Mesopotamian religion was the goddess of war and love. She was also the goddess of rain and thunderstorms, thus her association with An, the sky god—and was pictured with the lion,

whose roar resembled thunder. Ishtar also symbolized feminine characteristics, physically and emotionally, so she loved, betrayed, danced, laughed, deceived, married and beautified the whole universe and the sky, (Iraqi author and researcher Zaid Khaldon Gamil.)

Ishtar, represented by doves, was also the goddess of fertility and was revered all around. As Ishtar rose in prominence, she became central in Babylonian and Sumerian society, and so became the central figure in the Cult of Ishtar. Archaeologists identify evidence for these cults at Ebla, a town located in modern day Syria, highly influenced by the Cult of Ishtar; the evidence found in the town's religious temples could help archaeologists accurately describe the goddess and her worshippers.

The Ishtar Gate was the eighth gate leading to the inner city of Babylon. Built around 575 BC by King Nebuchadnezzar II, the gate was dedicated to the Babylonian goddess Ishtar. Hence its name. As part of the city walls of Babylon, the Ishtar Gate was one of the original Seven Wonders of the World.

CYBELE (1200 BCE)

Cybele was the only known goddess of Phrygia, an early Greek city-state, adopted by the Greek colonists of Asia Minor, before spreading to mainland Greece. She was often depicted either sitting upon a throne or in a chariot drawn by lions. An Earth goddess, she is connected to harvest, fertility, magic, and knowledge. Cybele was partially assimilated in later Greek pantheons by Gaia, Rhea, and Demeter, although she continued to be worshipped as an essentially foreign mystery-goddess.

A 2,100-year-old Cybele statue was found a few years ago at the site of Kurul Castle, in the northern Turkish province of Ordu. Cybele, the Anatolian mother goddess statue, is the most important piece found in the excavation.

Gaia
The primordial Greek Goddess

The Personification of Earth

Gaia was worshipped under the epithet "Anesidora", which means "giver of gifts. She is Mother Earth, power & energy, the life-giving source of this planet. The sky, seas & all creatures come from her womb. Gaia is the first mother or earth goddess and is one of the gods that ruled over the universe before anything existed, including the Titans. Myths indicate that Chaos existed before everything else; it consisted of Darkness, Mass, and Void, and then the Earth took the shape of Gaia, the Greek goddess.

Goddess Gaia, in the contemporary world is a new consciousness in us to strive for totality, wholeness, individuation and connection.

James Lovelock, in "Gaia: A New Look at Life on Earth "advanced a Gaia hypothesis stating that living organisms and inorganic material are part of a dynamic system that shapes the Earth's biosphere, maintains the Earth as a suitable environment for life. In some Gaia theory approaches, the Earth itself is viewed as an organism

with self-regulatory functions. Carl Jung advanced that the archetypal mother was a part of the collective unconscious of all humans, and various Jungian students (e.g. Erich Neumann and Ernst Whitmont) have stated that such mother imagery underpins several mythologies, and precedes the image of the paternal "father," in such religious systems. This helps to strengthen the universality of such mother goddess imagery around the world.

Adya Shakti
Parama Shakti/Adi Parashakti

The Mother Goddess, Mahadevi; The Cosmic Energy and The Divine Power; Supreme Being, Para Brahman (Shaktism)

Adya Shakti or Adi Shakti symbolizes 'primal power' or 'primal energy.' In Hinduism she represents the power

or energy infusing the whole existence, permeating all creation - animate, inanimate and the divine. All the other goddesses in the Hindu pantheon, are incarnations of Adya Shakti. She is the entity from which the universe has emanated, and the point where everything merges at the end.

"The Divine Mother's magic is as ancient as life itself. She existed before Gods and mortals, and she will still exist even after the great dissolution. Mother is pure energy in subtle form, but in times of need or just out of the desire to play, she manifests". (Elizabeth U Harding, Kali: The Black Goddess of Dakshineswar).

Adya Shakti is worshipped and celebrated in India and among Indians outside India in several forms. Some of these forms are pan-Indian, like Kali and Durga, while the others are local like Meenakshi Amman (Fish-eyed Mother) in Tamil Nadu, South India, Vaishno Devi (Goddess Vaishno) in Jammu and Kashmir, North India, Amba Devi in Gujarat, Western India and Attukal Amma (Mother Attukal), Kerala, South India.(Dianne Jennet, 'A Million Shaktis Rising: Pongala, a Women's Festival in Kerala, India')

Vach (vāc)
Vedic goddess personifying speech

The Rig Veda describes goddess Vac as one of the earliest divinities in the Hindu pantheon. She is the creative personification of ritual speech, the basis of cosmic-ritual order.

"She enters into the inspired poets and visionaries, gives expression and energy to those she loves; she is called

the "mother of the Vedas" and consort of Prajapati, the Vedic embodiment of mind."

(Holdrege, Barbara A. (2012-02-01). Veda and Torah: Transcending the Textuality of Scripture. SUNY Press. ISBN 978-1-4384-0695-4)

Elsewhere, such as in the Padma Purana, she is stated to be the wife of Vision (Kashyapa), the mother of Emotions, and the friend of Musicians (Gandharva).

(The Myths and Gods of India, Alain Daniélou, pages 260-261).

On one level, Mother Vak is sacred speech including the hymns and ritual chants. On another level she is also ordinary speech among ordinary people. She is far more than speech and includes the power of perceiving, grasping the nature of things, naming them, and expressing the perception with coherence and form. Her nature is subtle, eternal, imperishable, and above all incomprehensible.

(Russill Paul, The Yoga of Sound: Tapping the Hidden Power of Music and Chant (New World Library, 2004) page 70)

Aditi

('boundless' or 'innocence')

A Vedic goddess in Hinduism, she is the personification of the infinite, goddess of the earth, sky, unconsciousness, the past, the future and fertility. As a primeval goddess, she is considered the mother of many gods, including Vishnu in his dwarf incarnation and, in a later reappearance, Krishna. She supports the sky, sustains all existence, and nourishes the earth. It is in the latter sense that she is often represented as a cow.

The name is mentioned in Vedas as mother of Surya (Sun) and other celestial bodies - Adityas (meaning sons of Aditi).The first mention of goddess Aditi is found in

Rigveda, estimated to have been composed roughly during 1700-1100 BC. The name Aditi has the root "da" (to bind or fetter) and suggests that as A-diti, she is un-bound, free, and it is evident in the hymns that she is often invoked to free devotees from different hindrances, especially sin and sickness. (Mandala 2.27.14).

The mother goddess can be interpreted as expressing

ideas of power, autonomy and primacy in the widest sense. She conveys not so much the idea of physical motherhood but a world view in which the creative power of femininity is central; the goddess mediates between life and death and contains within herself the powerful possibility of regenerating herself over time. The Vedas describe her as the wife of Daksha, the grandfather of all living forms. But in the Puranas and epics she is depicted as deva matri, the mother of not just the Adityas, but all 330 million gods. In the Matsya Purana she appears in a brief role as the receiver of a pair of ear rings from Indra, the ruler of heavens, as a gift during the churning of the oceans. The Vishnu Purana describes her as the daughter of Daksha and the wife of Kashyapa, the progenitor of human race.

The Devi Bhagavata portrays her as Devaki, the mother of Lord Krishna, in an earthly manifestation of Aditi. In the Puranas Aditi has an opponent in the form of Diti (the bound one), who is the mother of daityas or asuras, a type of demons.

Amari De | De Develeski
Romani Goddess

Goddess Amari De's themes are art, humour, relationships, love, fertility, wealth, health and beauty. Her symbol is light. In Romania, Amari De is worshipped as a Romani Goddess, the great mother of all things and the personification of nature. Myths and folklore hold that She bestows wealth, health, beauty, love, fertility and insight to those who seek her. Descriptions elaborate that a divine light always shone from Her face.

"The Romanies came originally from the East, probably from India...The Romanies, too, believe in the Great Mother, Amari De or De Develeski, the personification of Nature. Devel or Duvel derives from the Sanskrit word Deva."(Robertson: Communion with the Goddess)

Cunda

Female Boddhisatva

Often referred to as the "Mother of the Buddhas", she is also known as Chundi, Cundi or Chunda. While Cundī is lesser known in Tibetan Buddhism, she is revered in East Asian Buddhism. In China, she is known as Zhuntí Púsà. Brahminic mythology, identified as a vindictive form of Durgā, or Pārvatī, before being syncretized into Buddhism. The first literature source of Cundī and the Cundī Dhāranī is the Kārandavyūhasūtra, a sūtra centered around the bodhisattva Avalokiteśvara. Cundī is depicted with eighteen arms, each wielding implements that symbolize upaya, representing the eighteen merits of attaining Buddhahood as described in Cundī Dhāranī Sūtra. She is kindly to the good but terrifying to the wicked. However, for a worshipper who regards her, her hands are in a position of teaching and charity.(Storm Rachel, Indian Mythology).Relief from Central India, 10th Century.

Vinayaki

Vinayaki is the elephant-headed goddess, the female avatar of Ganesha, also considered as one of the Shakti's or yoginis of Parvati.

Vināyakī is an elephant-headed Hindu Goddess. She is known by various names — Vainayaki, Gajanani (elephant-faced), Vighneshvari (Mistress) and Ganeshani. These identifications have defined her as the shakti of Ganesha.(Mundkur)

A unique representation of Vinayaki is found in the tantric seat of worship, the Chausathi Yogini temple, Hirapur, Odisha. Here, she symbolizes one of the 64 Yoginis, a sacred feminine force. In a shrine of the Thanumalayan temple, Kanyakumari is the stone sculpture of a reticent, little-known goddess. Seated cross-legged in Sukhasana, this four-armed goddess has a battle-axe in her upper-left hand and a conch in the lower left hand. In her two right hands, she carries a vase and a staff, around which she entwines her long trunk. She is the venerated female elephant-headed goddess, Vinayaki or Ganeshini, whose origins have been ignored by most writings on Hindu mythology. This collage also contains the image of Gajananaa, from the yogini temple at Ranipur Jharial.

Varuni

The Indian goddess of wine
Varuni, She-Who-Encompasses.
V*RUNE
Alternate meaning: {She-Who-Obliterates}

The meaning of Her name is probably connected with the Sanskrit madhu, 'honey'. Related Sanskrit words seem to be Madyam, 'intoxicating liquor', used in worship of the Shakti's, Divine-Energies, and Madugha, a plant yielding a honey-like substance used in making love spells and in nuptial ceremonies; it is chewed by debators to ensure success, the same concept expressed in the

English phrase: 'honey-tongued'. In this picture, she is accompanying her husband Varuna, the god associated with skies and the seas. Varuni, also known as Varunani is described in Rigveda. She emerged from the *Samudra manthan*, during churning of the *Amrita*.

Nava Durga's of Navaratri

Day 1: Goddess Shailaputri

Hindu mythology states that Goddess Shailputri was born after Goddess Sati's self-immolation. Also famous as Parvati, the daughter of Himalaya, Goddess Shailputri is venerated on the first day of the Navratri across the country.

Mostly depicted as riding a bull, she holds a trident in one hand while on the other, a lotus flower. Also referred to as 'Hemavati', she is considered the most important of all the nine forms of Durga. Like Goddess Sati, Shailputri, too, is married to Lord Shiva.

Day 2 - Goddess Brahmacharini

The Dwitiya Tithi is dedicated to the Brahmacharini Avatar of Durga. She is the unmarried form of the Mother Goddess. Adorned in a white saree, she holds a *Kamandal* and a *Japa mala* in the left and the right hand respectively. Convinced by Rishi Narada, Goddess Durga accepted Lord Shiva as her husband and observed severe austerity. Consequently, she came to be known by the name of Brahmacharini or Tapashcharini after thousands of years of penance.

Day 3 - Goddess Chandraghanta

Om Devi Chandraghantayai Namah

Day three of Navratri, i.e. Tritiya, is meant for worshipping Maa Chandraghanta. With a third eye that opens during times of war, this form of Goddess Durga protects her devotees from evil, and so she is seen equipped with myriad weapons.

The pictorial depiction

portrays her with ten hands, and mounted on a tiger. Armed with a trident (Trishul), a mace (gada), a sword (talwar), a pitcher (kamandal) in the left side and a lotus, a bow, an arrow and Japa mala in the right, she holds the vara mudra and the Abhaya mudra in the other two hands, respectively.

Day 4: Goddess Kushmanda

On the fourth day, the Goddess Kushmanda (popularly known as Devi Ashta Bhuja) is worshipped. Devi Kushmanda is a form of Goddess Durga, the creator of the universe. She is a Hindu goddess, believed to have created the world with her divine smile. Her name signifies her role: Ku means 'a little', Ushma means 'warmth' or 'energy' and Anda means 'cosmic egg'.

Day 5: Goddess Skandamata

Goddess Parvati is worshipped as Skandamata on the fifth day of Navratri, Maa Skandamata is depicted as sitting on a ferocious lion with baby Karthikeya, her elder son. She has four hands, two upper hands carrying Lotus flowers, her lower right hand cradling baby Karthikeya and her lower left hand in Abhaya Mudra. Baby Karthikeya is also named Skanda, hence Goddess Parvati in this form is known as Skandamata (mother of Lord Skanda).

Day 6 : Goddess Katyayani

Goddess Katyayani is worshipped on the sixth day. Famed as the fierce one, Katyayani is the warrior form of Goddess Parvati. Goddess Sati was born in the house of sage Katya and the name originates from this connection. Hindu mythology elucidates that this form of the warrior Goddess was adopted in order to kill the demon Mahishasura. This avatar of Adishakti sits on a ferocious lion, having three eyes, and four hands. Two of her left hands are carrying a lotus, and a sword, while her two right hands are seen in Varada and Abhaya Mudra respectively.

Day 7 :Goddess Kaalratri

Devi Kalratri is revered as one of the many destructive forms of Maa Shakti which includes Kali, Mahakali, Bhadrakali, Bhairavi, Mrityu, Rudrani, Chamunda, Chandi and Durga. She is mounted on a donkey and has four hands, two of which carry a torch and sword, while the other two show gestures of protection.

Day 8 : Goddess Mahagauri

On the auspicious day of Maha Ashtami, devotees worship Goddess Mahagauri. The term Gauri symbolizes her as the daughter of Giri or mountain. The Devi rides on a bull and is has four arms through which she relays fear and power with a trident. She holds a tambourine in her left upper arm and the lower one is in the form of a blessing.

Day 9: Goddess Siddhidatri

On the Navami Tithi, the form of Durga that is worshipped is known as Siddhidatri. She is the manifestation of the formless Adishakti, who is worshipped by Lord Shiva himself. The pictorial depiction of the Mother Goddess shows her seated on a fully-bloomed pink lotus. This form of Shakti signifies knowledge, wisdom and accomplishment. Her name also signifies perfection. Goddess Siddhidhatri embodies the eight siddhis residing in her - Anima, Mahima, Garima, Laghima, Prapti, Prakamya, Ishitva, and Vashitva.

Dharani Penu
Earth Goddess of the Kondh Tribe

Regarded as the divine creator of agriculture, born from the underworld, the goddess is believed to have created the buffalo, the most sacred sacrificial animal. She protects her believers from pestilence, depravity and evil. Worshipped in all ceremonies, all rituals start with the name of Dharani Penu. She is responsible for growth, vegetation and product of land and so, is installed in a hut in the front yard of each village called Kudeli.

The Gramadevati of Sebatipur village
Kanas block, Puri

Gramadevata or Gramadevati is a chosen deity for the entire village or the rural setting whose primary duty is to 'safeguard' the interests of the villagers. People often have a special affection and gratitude towards the deity. Thus every family in the village has a special kind of emotional attachment or bonding towards the deity and the temple.

Many of these village deities are deprived of well-built temple structures and are found in the open under trees.

These rural goddesses are strong and masculine in nature, but some are maternal; few others powerful warriors and destroyers. Some goddesses are identified with wildlife, multifaceted, some are a personification of art, literature and culture. Bedecked with flowers, the Goddess holds her sway, oblivious to the anonymous, ancient temple close by.

Dakshina Chandi
Bhogapur, Khurda

A non-descript village and an anonymous temple steeped in history: Built in the khakhara order, it is similar to the Vaitala temple of Bhubaneswar and the Varahi temple of Chaurasi. The 'Dakshina Chandi' is a 13th century Eastern Ganga era architecture. A magnificent ten armed Mahishamardini Durga is worshipped as the presiding Goddess. Local beliefs attribute the temple to have been constructed during the reign of Ganga Monarch Langula Narasingha Deva.

The temple has a Vimana of Khakhara design and a rectangular Jagamohana of improvised Kalingan order. The sandstone temple structure was covered with cement during the last renovation drive initiated by a local named Pitabas Chhotarai.

Goddess Dakshina Chandi is one of the most popular and awe-inspiring deities who figures prominently in the cultural life of Odisha, Bengal and eastern India. The Tantric hymns that describe her iconic representations

show her as a fierce and destructive embodiment of the cosmic feminine. There is repeated stress on her uncanny visual attributes such as her fierce appearance, fanged mouth with a blood-stained lolling tongue, and severed limbs and skulls that form her adornments. The goddess possesses a female body but the features that define her stance and posture, such as trampling the supine body of Shiva, evoke destruction. In the early years of her pre-history, she was a tribal and folk deity. A goddess named Chandi, in the early stages of her development was part of the group of female divinities worshipped by rural Odias. These village goddesses, Gramadevatis, were represented with amorphous and crude stone images smeared in vermilion and found in villages. In this form, she is part of the rural collective religious beliefs, where goddesses were propitiated by animal sacrifices.

Goddess Jyestha

Jyestha is the goddess who embodies all that is inauspicious. As the embodiment of disease and poverty, she is worshipped to prevent such misfortunes. Here, she is seen enthroned, holding a blue lotus (nilotpala) and flanked by her crow-headed standard (dhvaja). Alongside sit her daughter and her bull-headed son, carrying a club. Jyestha is placated by devotees fearful of infant diseases; in eastern India she is specifically associated with smallpox. Her earliest appearance was in northern India in the fourth century;

According to the scriptures of Padma Purana, it is believed that when God and demons were churning the ocean for the nectar of immortality, various things came out of the womb of the ocean- precious gems, divine cows & horses. Devi Lakshmi also appeared out of the ocean and married Lord Vishnu. But before Devi Laksmi, Jyestha Devi came out of the ocean as a dark woman, wearing dirty clothes and carrying a broom and pan and this is how she became the elder sister of Devi Lakshmi. Unlike Devi Lakshmi, both Gods and Demons unwelcomed her due to her appearance and qualities, so she decided to dwell in inauspicious and dirty places.

She is usually depicted with a flabby belly, thick thighs, a large nose, hanging lower lip, and holding a broom; in short, depicted as the epitome of 'Ugliness'.

Mother Goddess of Indus Valley

The spontaneous need to combine the Divine with mother was probably man's earliest spiritual experience. The Indus inhabitants manifested their idea of the Supreme Divinity in Mother Earth that blessed them with grain, water, air, fire and shelter. The terracotta figurines of the Mother Goddess, recovered in excavations at various Indus sites (now mostly in Pakistan), are not only the earliest manifestations of the Divine Power in any medium but are also suggestive of a well evolved Mother Goddess worship cult. The figurines of the Goddess, datable from 3000 B. C. to the 1st century B. C., a primitive manifestation of the proto Mother in terracotta idols seems to have continued to prevail till almost the beginning of the Christian era. This is the iconic perception of the Being who is not only the protector but also symbolizes absolute aesthetic beauty, absolute motherhood and absolute womanhood.

"Astonishingly ornate, this terracotta figurine represents a female divinity now unanimously identified as the Mother Goddess, perhaps a votive image, people's reverence for the real birth-giving mother, or for the earth for all her bounties, was in the root of worshipping a deity who was primarily the 'mother' and a female in general. Otherwise also, the cult of female-worship, coupled with the fertility cult, seems to have been deep rooted in India's soil itself. The recovery of a large number of Mother Goddess figurines almost from every excavated site suggests that the Mother Goddess worship cult was very wide-spread during Indus days. The figurine has been cast with an elaborate headgear supported by a pair of bands and a brooch, tight-fitted short tunic with skirt part fastened with a broad waist-band using a medallion like clasp, and tight-fitted trousers, necklaces, ear-ornaments.

This large figurine from Mohenjo-Daro is an excellent example of the technical maturity of the Harappan artisans in clay modeling and baking.The fan-shaped headdress is like a large cup, which is hung on either side like oil-lamps or incense-trays. The figure is adorned with two necklaces, the smaller with a set of four cylindrical pendants, while the longer one hangs lower.

The eyes have been conceived with two round pellets of clay, and the nose as pinched." (Harappa.com)

Pic:Standing figure of the Mother Goddess
C. 2700-2100 B.C.
Place of Origin: Mohenjo-Daro
Materials: Terracotta

Hariti

Hārītī, Japanese Kishi-mojin, in Buddhist mythology, is a child-devouring ogress who is said to have been converted from her cannibalistic habits by the Buddha to become a protectress of children. The Buddha hid the youngest of her five hundred children under his begging bowl, and thus made her realize the sorrow she was causing other parents. Hārītī is usually represented surrounded by children or carrying a Child, a Pomegranate, or a Cornucopia. Her cult traveled north into Central Asia and China, where she is regarded as the special guardian of children and of women in childbirth, and to Japan, where she has sometimes been regarded with a feminine form of the protective deity, Kannon.

Hariti, the Goddess of Children is found in several sculptures. Study of Second and Third Century Sculptures of the Common Era from the Kushana Period shows many religious influences converging into the Iconography of this Goddess, duly connected with local Myths and Legends in the Cult belief of a Benevolent Mother Goddess.

A Sculpture seen in the British Museum, taken from Pakistan, belongs to 2-3rd Century CE and shows Hariti seated on a chair with a child on her lap and seven children gathered around her feet. These children are also believed to represent those from different geographical regions of that time.

The root of the name is interesting. "HAR" means stealing and thus "HARITI" means one who steals.

Many Hariti sculptures are seen in the Gandhara Region dating back to 2nd Century CE and also in Mathura and Guntur in Telengana. Hariti worship grew in popularity and till date her worship continues in Nepal, Japan etc.

Iconography of Hariti :-

How her Iconography evolved is interesting. Many Matruka sculptures from Hindu pantheon show a similar aspect of a kid in the lap. Similarly, in Helenistic Sculptures nursing women of small terracotta images have survived, suggesting a suitable connection. With the spread of Buddhism all over Asia upto Japan, the Goddess herself found a place of worship from Nepal to Tibet to Japan and other Far east countries.

In the Kathmandu Valley of Nepal, she is known as Hārītī Mā "Mother Hārītī", and her main temple is part of Kathmandu's Swayambhunath stupa complex. She is perceived as the consort of Pañcika and as protector of children, and is a patron of the Newar people of Kathmandu, Bhaktapur and Lalitpur District. The Newars call her Ajima, meaning "grandmother" in the Newar language.

In Japanese tradition, Kishimojin is an aspect of Kannon, the goddess of mercy, and she bears the epithets "Bringer of Happiness" and "Giver of Children and Easy Delivery". In Chinese Buddhism, Hārītī is also known as Hēlìdì or Hēlìdìmǒ. In Chinese tradition, she is one of the Twenty-Four Protective Devas as a group of Dharmapalas who are venerated as protectors of Buddhists and the Dharma. Statues of this group and Hārītī are often enshrined within the Mahavira Hall in Chinese temples and monasteries. Hārītī is a figure of the 26th chapter of the Lotus Sutra, and is especially important to Nichiren Buddhism. In Shingon Buddhism, she is named Karitei or Karitei-mo.

In Vinayapitaka, a Buddhist canton, Hariti is referred by the name "HUNASHI" which means joy. As per tales Hariti was an Yakshi and was married to Panchika, who was an Yaksha. With the spread of Buddhism, Hariti, along with her consort Panchika (Kubera) were worshipped from Kashmir in North India to down south (Hariti Shrines are seen in Gulbarga, Vishakhapatnam and Nagarjunakonda too), from Dacca in the East to Maharashtra in the West, as also in Ancient Gandhara, Nepal, Bali, Indonesia, China and Japan etc.

Source: Dr KP Ravichandran

ARANYANI

'Aranyani' is a Hindu goddess of the woods, forest and animals that dwell within them. Worshipped in India for centuries as a symbol of life and fertility, she governs the forests and is guardian of the animals.

Described as elusive and fond of quiet glades in the jungle, she is, however, fearless. She is a rarely seen deity, recognized in the sounds of the trees, particularly at dusk. Rigvedic hymns describe how she wanders so far from the fringe of civilization. There seems to be no temple dedicated to her.

This goddess is unique for two reasons. First, she hints at an archaic goddess known as the mistress of animals. Second, she sounds very much like the Yakshis of the later Indian tradition, female beings who dwell in the forest, are worshiped away from the village, and who have, despite their generally benign qualities, certain uncanny characteristics.

USHA

Ushas is a Vedic goddess of dawn in Hinduism. She frequently appears in the Rigvedic hymns.

Goddess Usha symbolizes dawn; she is the daughter of the sky, the creator of the light, who rouses all life. She stirs awake all creatures, and makes the birds of air fly up. Borne on a hundred chariots, she yokes her steed before the arrival of the sun and is never, ever late. Loved by the Asvins, sister of gods, she eludes the Sun who pursues her always. She is not just the harbinger of light but hope, happiness, wealth and all the good things. Goddess of light and beauty, whom the Rishis of ancient times invoked for their protection.

In contemporary Hinduism, the revered Gayatri mantra is a daily reminder of Ushas Sri Aurobindo states Ushas is "the medium of the awakening, the activity and the growth of the other gods; she is the first condition of the Vedic realization. By her increasing illumination the whole nature of man is clarified; through her [mankind] arrives at the Truth, through her he enjoys [Truth's] beatitude." An exalted goddess in the Rig Veda, she is less prominent in post-Rigvedic texts. She is often spoken of in the plural, "the Dawns."

Ushas is regionally worshipped during the festival of Chhath Puja, in Bihar and Uttar Pradesh, and in Nepal.

YAMUNA

(as Dwarapallika accompanied by a Gana)

Yamuna, the sacred river in Hinduism and the main tributary of the Goddess Ganga (Ganges) is considered the holiest river. The river is worshipped as a Hindu goddess called Yamuna. Yamuna is known as Yami in early texts, while in later literature, she is called Kalindi. In Hindu scriptures, she is daughter of Surya, the sun god, and Sanjna, cloud goddess. She is regarded as the twin sister of Yama, god of death. She is also associated with god Krishna as one of Ashtabharya, his consort as well and plays an important role in his early life as a river.

Photo from Halibasappa Temple,
Aihole, Karnataka
9th Century A.D.@India International Centre

The Sapta Matrikas

('Sapta, means Seven and 'Matrika' means Divine Mother)

The Sapta Matrikas are incarnations of Goddess Shakti (the goddess of power). They are namely - Brahmani, Maheshwari, Kaumari, Vaishnavi, Varahi, Indrani and Chamundi. In some places, the Matrikas are counted as eight (Ashta Matrikas) by including Narasimhi. Their references are found in ancient Puranas, such as Varaha Purana, Matsya Purana, Markandeya Purana etc. indicating their antiquity. Each of the mother goddesses (except for Chamunda) takes her name from a particular God: Brahamani form Brahma, Vaishnavi from Vishnu, Maheswari from Shiva, Kaumari from Skanda, Varahi from Varaha and Indrani from Indra. They are armed with the same weapons, wear identical ornaments, ride the same vahanas and also carry the same banners like their corresponding male Gods. The earliest reference of Sapta Matrika is found in Markandeya Purana and V.S Agarwalla dates it to 400 A.D to 600 A.D.

The Indian treasure of sculptures related to mother goddesses is rich with Sapta Matrikas. The Matrikas are idolized as caring and protective in their sculptures as against their frightening and ferocious depiction in the scriptures. The sculptures radiate reverence, not horror, though the associated symbolism and attributes of each Matrika are retained. This singular characteristic has been the mainstay of Sapta Matrika sculptures. This moderation of the ferocity of the Sapta Matrikas, when transferred from scripture to a sculpture is guided by the fact that art must look beautiful and hence something terrible is to be transformed into a likable figure. Moreover, every artist is inspired by his individual perception and to that extent, he is free to modify his original sources. The only exception is the two Matrikas, Chamunda who is always present as ferocious. even in art, and Varahi with a boar's face.

Statue from Kailashnathar temple.

Chamunda

"In order to defeat the darkness, you must bring it into the light."
Om Eim Hrim Kilm Chamundayei Vechei Namaha

Known popularly as Chamundeshwari, Chamundi or Charchika, Chamunda is a fearsome form of Chandi, the Hindu Divine Mother Shakti and is one of the seven Matrikas. Chamunda is one of the oldest known tantric deities and one of the chief yoginis, venerated in all Yogini temples.

Bhandarkar states that Chamunda was originally a tribal goddess, venerated by the tribals residing in the Vindhya mountains, Central India. It is held that the tribes

offered goddesses animal and human sacrifices along with rituals offering liquor. These methods of worship were retained in Tantric worship of Chamunda, even after assimilation into Hinduism. The fierce nature of this goddess is due to her association with Rudra (Shiva), identified with fire god Agni at times. Chamunda is included in the pantheon of the sapta-matrika.

The Matrikas are terrifying mother goddesses, abductors and eaters of children; i.e., they were emblematic of childhood pestilence, fever, starvation, and disease. They were propitiated in order to avoid those ills, that carried off so many children before they reached adulthood. (http://www.art-and-archaeology.com/india/jagat/jagat13.html). She is included in the Saptamatrika lists in ancient Hindu texts like the Mahabharata (Chapter 'Vana-parva'), the Devi Purana and the Vishnudharmottara Purana. She is often depicted in the Saptamatrika group in sculptures, examples of which are Ellora and Elephanta caves. Though she is always portrayed last (rightmost) in the group, she is sometimes referred to as the leader of the group. While other Matrikas are considered as Shaktis (powers) of male divinities and resemble them in their appearance, Chamunda is the only Matrika who is a Shakti of the great Goddess Devi rather than a male god. She is also the only Matrika who enjoys independent worship of her own; all other Matrikas are always worshipped together.

There are several Chamunda temples in Odisha. The 8th-century Vaitala Deula is the most prominent and one of the earliest temples in Bhubaneswar. The Mohini temple and Chitrakarini temple in Bhubaneswar are also dedicated to Chamunda. Kichakeshwari Temple, near Baripada and Charchika Temple, near Banki in Odisha enshrine forms of Chamunda.

Temple sculpture of the Tantric goddess Chamunda, 9th century, Madhya Pradesh British Museum.

According to legend, Chamunda appeared from the frown of the benign goddess Parvati to kill demons Chanda and Munda. Here, Chamunda is viewed as a form of Parvati. According to Matsaya Purana she, with other matrikas was created by Shiva to help him kill the demon Andhakasura, who has an ability, like Raktabija, to generate from his dripping blood. Chamunda with other matrikas drinks the blood of the demon ultimately helping Shiva kill him.

Ratnakara, in his text Haravijaya, also describes this feature of Chamunda, but solely credits Chamunda, not the other matrikas of sipping the blood of Andhaka. Having drunk the blood, Chamunda's complexion changed to blood-red. The text further says that Chamunda does a dance of destruction, playing a musical instrument whose shaft is Mount Meru, the spring is the cosmic snake Shesha and gourd is the crescent moon. She plays the instrument during the deluge that drowns the world.

Important temples are dedicated to her in Odisha: Mohini temple, Chitrakarini temple, Boitala (Vaital) temple(Bhubaneswar), Charchika temple(Banki), Kichakesvari temple(Mayurbhanja).

She is found in the following postures:
1) trailokyavijaya chamunda
2) vrishchikodari chamunda
3) chandrabhaga chamunda

Chamunda: Odisha State Museum   Ramachandi Temple, Puri   Gangeswari Temple, Puri

*Goddess Chamunda Broken statue
near Gajasimha Mandap, Bhogapur*

The original temple that housed Chamunda as the primary deity is now lost and replaced by a restored version. Though broken, the features of the staue are unmistakable. Chamunda is depicted as adorned by ornaments of bones and skulls. She wears a Yajnopavita (a sacred thread worn by Hindu priests) of skulls. She wears a jata mukuta, that is, headdress formed of piled, matted hair tied with snakes or skull ornaments. The goddess has an emaciated body and shrunken belly which shows protruding ribs and veins as well as bare teeth, protruding tongue and sunken eyes.

Brahmani

Yogini temples typically include sculptures of seven female goddesses known as matrikas ("mother-goddesses"). These feminized versions of Hindu gods are identifiable by the most common attributes of their male forms. Brahmani is the female version of Brahma. She is a form of Saraswati and is considered as the Shakti of the creator god Brahma in Hinduism. She is an aspect of Adi Shakti, possessing the "Rajas Guna" and is therefore the source of Brahma's power.

She has four heads and holds Brahma's prayer beads in her upper right hand, and his animal vehicle, the goose, is carved between her feet. Her hair, the matted locks of a renouncer, is piled high, and her left hand forms the wish-granting gesture; her missing right hand would have formed the gesture of reassurance.

Vaishnavi

Vaishnavi carries in one of her right hands the Chakra and in the left hand, the Sankha, her two other hands held in Abhaya and Varada Mudra respectfully. She wears a yellow garment and a Kirita Mukuta, adorned with the array of ornaments generally worn by Vishnu, and the element of her banner and Vahana is Garuda. The Vishnudharmotta Purana states she has six hands characterized by the Gada, Padma and Abhaya Mudra being held in the right hand, while left ones hold the Sankha, Chakra and Varada Mudra. In Devi-Purana she is represented as possessing four hands in which she carries Sankha, Chakra, Gada and Padma.

Maheswari

Maheshwari is one among the seven mother Goddesses or Sapta Matrikas. The Goddess Maheshwari is the power of god Shiva, also known as Maheshvara. Also known by the names Raudri, Rudrani and Maheshi, derived from Shiva's names Rudra and Mahesh, the vehicle or Vahana of Goddess Maheswari is Nandi (the bull). Usually depicted as having four arms – two arms in Varada Mudra (granting wishes) and one in Abhaya Mudra (protection) and two arms depicted as holding the Sula (lance) and Akshamala or a Damaru, she has an interesting iconography. The white complexioned, Trinetra (three eyed) Goddess holds similar weapons to Shiva and has numerous other symbols and characteristics of Shiva: when she is depicted with six arms, she carries a Trishula (trident), Damaru (drum), Akshamala (a garland of beads), Panapatra (drinking vessel) or axe or an antelope or a kapala (skull bowl) or a serpent and is adorned with serpent bracelets; Sometimes she is shown wearing a crescent moon and the *jatā mukuta* (a headress formed of piled, matted hair). In some very rare images, Goddess Maheshwari is depicted as having five faces. "In the scheme of the Khadgamala, each of these Eight Mothers represent a human passion that must be overcome and controlled before we can enter further into Sri Chakra. We worship each passion as an aspect of Devi, then internalize it; and when we internalize each deity, we 'become' Her, so that She is not separate from us. In that way, we 'conquer' each passion."

Kaumari

(at Kandariya MahadevaTemple)
Khajuraho, Madhya Pradesh

One among the 'Sapta Matrikas' (Seven Mothers), Kaumari is associated with Skanda. Here, she rides on Skanda's Peacock. The rest of the Matrikas are displayed on niches surrounding the base in the temple.

Indrani

Indrani (Indrani-Indra's queen), also known as Shachi, is the queen of the devas in Hinduism. Described as very beautiful, proud and kind, she is the daughter of the asura Puloman and the consort of the king of the devas, Indra. Indrani (or Aindri) is also one of the Sapta Matrika's—the seven divine mothers. She is an important goddess in Shaktism, a major sect of Hinduism.

Matrika Indrani is described as being red, with three eyes and four hands. Two of her hands are found to be in Varada and Abhaya mudra, while the other two hands hold a vajra (thunderbolt) and a spear. She wears a crown on her head and is decorated with various ornaments. Her vahana, as well as her emblem banner, is an elephant. According to the Vishnudharmottara, like Indra, Indrani is yellow and has one thousand eyes. Indrani is associated with the kalpaka tree; sometimes, a lion is mentioned as her vahana.

Varahi

A long-cherished dream come true event was my visit to the Varahi Temple at Chaurasi, a famous Shakta shrine of the Prachi Valley of Odisha. I am glad that I chose a May afternoon as I had the temple all to myself. It was scorching hot but a gentle breeze started blowing soon after I arrived and the coconut trees all around created a magical web of light and shade. Famous as the beauty of the Prachi Valley, careful restoration work has been done here. The temple is dedicated to Goddess Varahi, the female counterpart of Varaha, the boar incarnation of Vishnu. One among the Sapta-matrikas group of Vaishnavi, Maheswari, Brahmani, Indrani, Kaumari and Chamunda, this is a rare temple dedicated to Varahi alone. Varahi is an incarnation of Bhu Devi. In Nepal, she is called Barahi. Varahi is worshipped by three practices of Hinduism: Shaivism (devotees of Shiva), Vaishnavism (devotees of Vishnu), and especially Shaktism (goddess worship). She is usually worshipped at night, using secretive Vamamarga Tantric practices. The Buddhist goddesses Vajravārāhī and Marichi have their origins from the Hindu goddess Varahi.

There are intricate carvings all over the temple walls, with number of erotic panels suggesting tantric rites. The Varahi temple of Chaurasi is decorated with both cult images as well as non-iconic figures. The central niches of the bada houses the parshvadevata images of Ganesha and Surya. The images of Surya and Ganesha are the parshvadevatas of western (back) and southern sides of the bada respectively. I spent the entire afternoon by myself till a group of young boys came to shoot their reels for social media. They said they liked the isolated temple and often used it as a backdrop to their songs. The temple was locked and as I strained through the barred door to have a glimpse of the Goddess, the gardener got a key and allowed me to enter the sanctum sanctorum. The life-size image of Varahi was so captivating!

Varahi, one of the Mother Goddesses, a manifestation of 64 Yoginis and the counterpart of Varaha-Vishnu was created to annihilate powerful demons like Chanda, Munda, Sumbha, Nisumbha, Raktavirjya and the tripuravijayi Mahisasura. The goddess Varahi is associated with the other mothers-Brahmani, Maheswari, Koumari, Vaisnavi, Indrani and Chamunda assisted Ambika in her combat against the demons.

A life-size image of Varahi (6 ft. 1 in. high and 2 ft. 9 in. wide) is enshrined in the temple at Chaurasi in Prachi valley in perfect state of preservation. Seated in lalitasana on a cushion placed on a plain legged seat with her hanging right leg resting on a life-like buffalo, the figure holds in her right hand a fish and in the left a blood-cup. Adorned with finger rings, anklets, valayas, armlets, necklace, large ear studs and a tiara over the hair which rises upwards in spiral coils, the three-eyed deity is pot-bellied and is clad in a dhoti. The plain halo is oval, the back of the figure is cut out of the oblong back-slab. The temple enshrining the image of Varahi comes in the order of Khakhara and bears resemblance to the Gouri temple at Bhubaneswar. On stylistic grounds, the temple and the image are assignable to the early part of 10th century A.D. In the Jagamohana of the temple are two loose sculptures of Varahi seated in Maharajalilasana, having a skull cup and a fish in two hands. The other is four armed holding in the lower left a skull cup, in the upper left a rosary, a water-pot in the lower right (upper left broken) associated with the mount buffalo and kneeling devotee. These two images were probably enshrined in some other temples in the locality. Varahi is believed to be the Shakti of Varaha. In the Tantric text 'Varahi Tantra' mention has been made of five forms of Varahi i.e., Svapna Varahi, Canda Varahi, Mahi Varahi (Bhairavi), Krcca Varahi and Matsya Varahi. The description of Matsya Varahi closely corresponds to the image enshrined in the temple. Apart from the erotic sculptures all over the temple walls, there are several decorative motifs-attractive Salabhanjikas and bajramastakas, battle scenes of Ramayana and the imposing Naga stambhas.

Aparajita

The female deity Aparajita is a significant Goddess in the Buddhist pantheon. According to the Buddhist sacred text Sadhanamala, there is a theory about her emergence from earth. So she is considered to be the manifestation of mother Earth and enthroned on lotus! Her complexion is bright too! It is believed that when monks focus in meditation, she protects them from evil powers, specially Mara. Aparājitā refers to one of the emanations of Ratnasambhava, as mentioned in the 5th-century Sādhanamālā (a collection of sādhana texts that contain detailed instructions for rituals). Her Colour is yellow; her identification mark is 'trampling upon Ganeśa'; her Mudrā is the capetadāna (slapping). The Nālandā fragment showing only the lower half of the full image is identified with that of Aparājitā. In it, the figure to the right of the principal goddess appears to be Indra and the rod held by him seems to be the handle of the parasol required to be held over her head by the gods beginning with Brahmā. The upper part of the Nālandā image

is unfortunately lost. Had it been complete, it would have been possible to find the capetadanā-mudrā in the right hand of the goddess and the noose with the raised index finger in the left, and a parasol over her head in continuation of the broken handle. This identification was confirmed when subsequently the Indian Museum image was discovered. This image is only slightly mutilated but is complete, and resembles the Nālandā fragment in the lower portion, while the whole image follows with precision, the directions given in the Sādhana quoted above. (Indian Buddhist Iconography)

Statues of Goddess Aparajita have been located at Ratnagiri, Odisha. In one image, the two-armed seated Goddess tramples the head of an elephant, an interesting depiction of the elephant as an "obstacle".

Pratyangira Devi

Goddess Pratyangira is associated with the Atharva Veda as its guardian goddess. Hence she is also known as Atharvana Bhadra Kali guarding over the secret mantras, tantras and yantras. Another name of the Atharva veda is Atharv Angirasa which denotes black magic or witchcraft. Angirasa kalpa denotes a manual on witchcraft. Prati-Angirasa denotes counter-witch craft. Thus, Devi Pratyangira is the one who reverses any black magic attack and Pratyangira sadhana is done mainly to protect oneself from attacks of black magic. Pratyangira has been described variously in various Tantras. Nikumbala Devi, who was worshipped by Indrajit, Ravana's son, is none other than Devi Pratyangira. Meru Tantra, Mantra Mahodadhi and several other texts mention the worship of this fierce goddess. She is described as a goddess with a male lion's face and a female human body representing the union of Shiva and Shakti. This combination of lion and human forms represents the balance of good and evil.

In Shaktism, Pratyangira is Siddhilakshmi, a form of Guhya Kali. In Vaishnavism, she is Narasimhi, the power of Narasimha avatar. In the Durga tradition, the Goddess is Purna Chandi, the fiery destructive power of Brahman. In the Vedas, Pratyangira is Atharvana Bhadrakali, the goddess of Atharva

Veda and magical spells. Pratyangira is also worshipped in Vajrayana Buddhism by the name of 'Simhamukha Dakini'. She holds a very prominent place in Vajrayana Buddhism as she is believed to be one of the personal deities of their first Guru Padmasambhava.

Tantra classifies deities as Shanta (calm), Ugra (wrathful), Prachanda (horrifying), Ghora (terrifying) and Teevra (ferocious). Pratyangira is considered as a Teevra Devata. Goddess Pratyangira is mainly described in two forms. One, the commonly seen form of the Goddess with four hands, seated on a lion. The other one is a greater form called Maha Pratyangira Devi with multiple faces of lions and numerous hands. Several Shakta texts also describe other forms like Aghora Pratyangira, Baggala Pratyangira, Lakshmi, Narayani Pratyangira, Pancha-Vimsatyakshari etc. (References: Max Muller (1897), 'The Hymns of the Atharva-Veda: The Sacred Books of the East'.}

Vajrayogini

Vajrayogini is a female Buddhist deity, consort of Heruka, a Dākinī (energetic being in female form) whose essence is great passion to free all from the shackles of selfishness and illusion. She is the manifestation of all Buddhas. Her red-colored body symbolizes the blazing of her tummo (candali) or "inner fire" of spiritual transformation as well as life force (Shakti). This Tantric Buddhist goddess works towards achieving greater well-being for others and to destroy ego in people. Adorned with various ornaments, she is often depicted in red, performing her proud, powerful, fearless and erotic dance. The curved knife she carries functions as an object that cuts through defilements, ignorance and stupidity. The cup she holds represents what in Sanskrit is known as 'Manasukha' or 'the great bliss'. She provides people who possess great passion, a way to transform it into enlightened virtues. In Nepal, the temple of Vajrayogini, sacred to both Buddhists and Hindus is situated in Sankhu, approximately 20 kilometers northeast of Kathmandu. The temple is also known as Bodhisattva's Temple. Vajrayogini ranks first and most important among the Dakinis. She is the 'Sarva-buddha-dakini' or simply the Dakini 'Who is the Essence of all Buddhas'. (Source : Cultural Nepal)

Gauri

Goddess Gauri or Parvati, the consort of Shiva is an avatar of Devi. Known to be gentle and nurturing, she is associated with beauty. Her radiance is in direct contrast to her alter ego Goddess Kali, who is dark and of fierce disposition. It is believed that once Lord Shiva, in a lighter vein, rebuked Parvati for being too dark. This upset the Goddess and she decided to do austere penance to acquire a fair complexion. She went to the dense

Sculpture shows Goddess Gauri sitting on a lizard Sri Hoysaleswara temple, Halebidu, Karnataka

forest and performed severe austerities for hundreds of years. Shiva's counterpart, Lord Brahma was immensely pleased with Parvati's penance and blessed her with a lustrous golden complexion and she came to be known as Gauri. This resplendent color of the Goddess came to be associated with fertility and plenty, while also representing a bountiful harvest.

ILA

Ila, a deity in Hindu pantheon, is known for her gender fluidity. As a man, he is known as Ila or Sudyumna and as a woman, is called Ilā. Ilā is considered the chief progenitor of the Lunar dynasty of Indian kings – also known as the Aillas ("descendants of Ilā").Ila is usually described as a daughter or son of Vaivasvata Manu and thus the sibling of Ikshvaku, the founder of the Solar Dynasty. In versions in which Ila is born female, she changes into a male form by divine grace soon after her birth. After mistakenly entering a sacred grove as an adult, Ila is either cursed to change his/her gender every month or cursed to become a woman. As a woman, Ilā married Budha, the god of the planet Mercury and the son of the lunar deity Chandra (Soma), and bore him a son called Pururavas, the father of the Lunar dynasty. After the birth of Pururavas, Ilā has transformed into a man again and fathered three sons.

In the Vedas, Ilā is praised as Idā, goddess of speech, and described as the mother of Pururavas.

The tale of Ila's transformations is told in the Puranas as well as the Indian epic poems, the Ramayana and the Mahabharata. A rare feature of the ancient Hindu religious tradition is the significance of goddess worship. A great number of goddesses are known in the earliest Hindu scriptures, the Vedic hymns. No other living religious tradition displays such an ancient, continuous, and diverse history of goddess worship.

Ratri

Ratri is a Vedic goddess connected with night. She is also called the 'Goddess of Night', 'Guardian of Night' or the 'Hindu Night-time Goddess'. The sister of Ushas, she ensures peaceful and sound sleep. She is depicted as a beautiful maiden in a star studded black coat, the one who strengthens vital power and a powerful mother. She is called glorious and immortal and is praised for providing light in the darkness. Pictured as benign, she is lauded for giving rest to all creatures and for bestowing life-sustaining dew. She is especially invoked to protect people from dangers peculiar to the night. Her abode is heaven. Cyclic rhythmic patterns of the cosmos in which light and darkness follow each other, are represented by her.

Chapter 4

The Dasamahavidyas

The Mahavidyas (great revelations or manifestations), are a group of ten goddesses who are mentioned in the Hindu literary tradition. Some of the goddesses in this group are individually important and date back to a much earlier time (Kali, for example), but the group appears to be a medieval-iconographic and mythological expression of an aspect of Mahadevi theology. In the Mahadevi theology, the Devi manifests herself in a great variety of forms.

The ten Mahavidyas are probably a Sakta version of Vishnu's ten avataras who appear from time to time to maintain the order of dharma. The Guhyatiguhya-tantra gives a list of the Mahavidyas and identifies each one with an avatara of Vihsnu, stating that these avataras arose initially from the different Mahavidyas. The origin of the ten Mahavidyas in Hindu mythology takes place in the context of the story of Sati and Shiva. Sati's father, Daksha, decides to perform a sacrifice and invites all inhabitants of the heavenly spheres to attend. The only couple he does not invite are Shiva and Shati. Daksha does not like his son-in-law because of Shiva's uncivilized habits and dishevelled appearance and so does not invite him. Siva is not offended but his wife Sati is greatly insulted and announces to Shiva that she would go to the sacrifice to disrupt it. Shiva forbids her and so Sati, after futile attempts to convince him. eventually loses her temper. First she assumes a dreadful form and then multiplies herself into ten forms, the Mahavidyas: Kali, Tara, Chinnamasta, Bhuvanesvari, Bagala, Dhumavati, Kamala, Matangi, Sodasi, and Bhairavi. The ten forms that Sati takes are not consistently described, and some of the forms, such as Kali and Tara, have several manifestations. (Kingsley)

The Dasa Mahavidyas or the ten great wisdom goddesses are significant in contemporary religious worship for several reasons.

Firstly, the Dasa Mahavidyas represent different aspects of the divine feminine and the power of consciousness. The worship of these goddesses is believed to help individuals connect with their inner selves, awaken their spiritual potential, and cultivate wisdom and insight. Their worship is also believed to help individuals overcome obstacles and challenges in their lives, and find balance and harmony within themselves and with the world around them.

Secondly, the Dasa Mahavidyas are associated with different mantras and yantras, which are powerful tools for spiritual practice and transformation. Mantras are sacred words or phrases that are repeated to invoke the power and blessings of the deity. Yantras are geometric designs that are used for meditation and visualization. The use of mantras and yantras associated with the Dasa Mahavidyas is believed to help individuals achieve spiritual growth and transformation.

Thirdly, the worship of the Dasa Mahavidyas is often associated with specific rituals, pujas, and festivals, which are an important part of Hindu religious practice. These rituals and festivals are often community-based and bring people together to celebrate and honor the divine feminine and the power of consciousness. The worship of the Dasa Mahavidyas is also seen as a way to promote social and environmental justice, as these goddesses are associated with compassion, wisdom, and transformation.

Finally, the worship of the Dasa Mahavidyas has been adapted and reinterpreted in contemporary contexts, such as the feminist movement, new age spirituality, and alternative healing practices. The goddesses are seen as symbols of female empowerment and liberation, and their worship is often used as a way to challenge patriarchal norms and values. Dasa Mahavidyas are significant in contemporary religious worship for their association with the divine feminine, spiritual growth and transformation, and community-based rituals and festivals. Their worship is a powerful way to connect with the inner self, cultivate wisdom and insight, and promote social and environmental justice

Kali

Goddess Kali is a prominent deity in Hinduism, known for her fierce and powerful nature. The Dasa Mahavidyas, or the Ten Wisdom Goddesses, represent various aspects of cosmic knowledge and power. Kali is one of the Mahavidyas and represents the primordial energy of transformation and dissolution.Each Mahavidya embodies a specific aspect of the divine feminine and has her own distinct iconography, mantras, and rituals. Kali, as one of the Mahavidyas, represents the fierce aspect of the goddess and is worshipped for her transformative powers and the destruction of negative energies.

Evolution of Goddess Kali:

The origin and evolution of Goddess Kali can be traced back to ancient Hindu scriptures and mythology. Kali is often associated with the goddess Durga, as her ferocious form. In the Devi Mahatmya, a text from the Markandeya Purana, Kali emerges from the forehead of the goddess Durga during a battle against the demon Raktabija. Kali's appearance is described as black or blue-skinned, adorned with a garland of skulls, and wielding various weapons in her multiple arms.Over time, Kali evolved into an independent deity, celebrated for her fierce nature and as the ultimate symbol of time, destruction, and transformation. She is associated with the dissolution of the ego, the destruction of ignorance, and the awakening of spiritual consciousness.

Iconography of Goddess Kali:

Goddess Kali is typically depicted as a fierce and terrifying figure. Her most common iconographic details include:

Dark or blue-black complexion: The color symbolizes her transcendence of the physical world and represents the infinite void or space from which all creation arises.

Naked form: Kali is often portrayed as naked, symbolizing her freedom from societal norms and attachments.

Multiple arms: She is depicted with multiple arms, usually four or eight, which symbolize her ability to perform multiple actions simultaneously.

Garland of skulls: Kali wears a garland made of human skulls, representing the cycle of life, death, and rebirth.

Severed heads and weapons: Her multiple hands hold various weapons, such as a sword, trident, and severed heads, symbolizing her power to destroy and overcome obstacles.

Rites and Rituals associated with Kali worship:

Worship of Goddess Kali involves various rites and rituals, which may vary in different regions and traditions. Here are some common elements of Kali worship:

Mantras and chants: Devotees recite Kali mantras and chants, such as the powerful "Om Krim Kalikayai Namah," to invoke her presence and blessings.

Offerings: Offerings made to Kali often include red hibiscus flowers, incense, fruits, sweets, and blood-red liquids like wine or pomegranate juice.

Animal sacrifices: In some traditional forms of Kali worship, particularly in rural areas, animal sacrifices are performed. However, it's important to note that such practices are not universally followed and are increasingly discouraged.

Tantric practices: Kali worship is often associated with tantric practices that involve meditation, visualization, and the awakening of Kundalini energy.

Kali Temples in India: There are several temples dedicated to Goddess Kali across India. Some of the notable Kali temples include:

Dakshineswar Kali Temple, Kolkata: Located on the banks of the Hooghly River, this temple is famous for its association with Sri Ramakrishna Paramahamsa, a renowned 19th-century mystic.

Kalighat Kali Temple, Kolkata: Situated in Kolkata, this temple is considered one of the holiest places of worship for Kali devotees.

Kamakhya Temple, Guwahati: Although primarily dedicated to the goddess Kamakhya, this temple complex in Assam also has a shrine dedicated to Kali.

Tarapith Temple, West Bengal: This temple in Birbhum district is regarded as one of the Shakti Peethas (sacred sites associated with the goddess Shakti) and is a popular pilgrimage site for Kali worshippers.

These are just a few examples, as Kali temples can be found in various other regions of India, each with its own unique significance and rituals associated with Kali worship. Goddess Kali has evolved as a fierce and transformative deity in Hindu mythology.

Tara

Among the Ten mahavidyas of the goddesses, Tara is the second. The deity plays a significant role in the Shakta Tarntric traditions of Hinduism and Vajrayana Tantric traditions of Buddhism. The connection of Tara with both Buddhism and Hinduism seems to be very interesting. Referring to Tara as Buddharupa has a major significance in Vajrayana Buddhism. The Buddhist Mahachinakrama Tara is iconographically identical to the one of several existing forms described in the Tarakula tantras. Tara in Buddhism is the supreme goddess of wellbeing of all sentient creatures across different universe systems. She is known as the loving mother, the protector, the swift one, wise one, wrathful one and also the peaceful one, mother of all Buddhas and who herself is the Boddhisatva and the granter of all boons.

The Goddess has 108 names. Thus she is referred to as Buddharupa and also Buddhajanani. MahachinaTara is also known in Buddhist Tantric literature as UgraTara, and the Vajrayogini temple at Śānku in Nepal, contains in the sanctum a figure of the terrible Ugratara. In this painting, the face of Tara is depicted with all her belongings like the khadga (sword), scimitar (katari) , kapala  (skull vessel for drinking), blue lotus, tiger skin garment, human head necklace and headdress. The hooded snake represents her Bhairava Akshobhya. The word "Hung" written tibetan represents the goddess herself residing over the white lotus.

Bhuvaneshwari

Bhuvanesvari, (fourth of the Ten Mahavidyas) embodies and controls the cosmos. Mythologically, she was created when the sun god, Surya, after having soma from the rishis, created the three worlds (the ancestral, human, and godly planes). Bhuvanesvari was created as a guardian of these worlds. She is considered part of the world or the world itself, both a source of creation and creation personified. She is queen of the cosmos. From her the world was created, and will be returned to at the end of the cycle. She is the mother of Brahma, Visnu, and Siva. Bhuvanesvari is particularly associated with the earth and creation, and provides the energy needed for existence and life. She is believed to embody each of the five elements (bhutas), and to have an intimate connection to the physical world (prakrti). Bhuvanesvari can manifest as mountains, stars,  rivers, anything; she is pervasive in the physical world. She is also known as Bhuvana (Mistress of the World), Sarvesi (Mistress of All), Sarvarupa (She Whose Form is All), and Visvarupa (She Whose Form is the World), to name a few. Unlike some of the other Mahavidyas, Bhuvanesvari did not have a wide-spread cult or following prior to be incorporated as one of the Ten.

Bhuvanesvari is beautiful, with a smiling face, flowing black hair, and a golden complexion. Sometimes, she is described as having a red, or bluish pallor. Her features are feminine: a small nose, large eyes, and full red lips. Her breasts are full and leaking milk, emphasising the motherly role she plays in the cosmos. In one myth Siva grew a third eye so that he could appreciate her beauty more. Her smiling and gentle demeanour is in contrast to some of the other Mahavidyas, such as Kali. They are still beautiful, but they are more fearsome; depicted as standing on corpses, wearing garlands of human heads, or naked and covered in blood. All the Mahavidyas are fearsome, but this aspect is stressed as a key feature in some and not in others. Kali, Tara, Bagala, Dhumavati, and Chinnamasta are always described as terrible, frightening, and fierce. The formidable nature of Tripura-sundari, Bhairavi, Matangi, and Bhuvanesvari is mentioned, but not much emphasis is placed on this feature. Only Kamala is regarded as benevolent.

Bhuvanesvari's beauty is said to reflect the beauty of creation and the physical world. She is gracious and kind, giving the world all it needs to survive. She protects creation and fights against sources of disorder, restoring the cosmic balance so that the world may thrive. Bhuvanesvari is said to have developed a third eye to better watch over creation. Often, she will appear as different manifestations to slay demons and restore balance. Bhuvanesvari is depicted with a noose and goad; both symbols suggest control. Some believe that she uses the goad for discipline and to control evil emotions such as anger, lust, and obsession. The noose symbolizes the barriers that keep us from knowing our true selves (atman), and by proxy, attaining liberation. However, countless interpretations exist. Her other two hands convey gestures of fearlessness and conferring boons. She also appears with a red lotus and a jewelled bowl, symbolizing growth and wealth. Not surprisingly, worship of Bhuvanesvari is believed to bring the devotee material wealth and spiritual well-being. She is seated on a lotus, a position of power with connotations of creation. In another creation myth, Brahma is depicted sitting on a lotus flower growing out of Visnu's navel. The lotus symbolises power, purity, and transcendence. Also, a crescent moon is present on her forehead, believed to symbolize replenishment, the endless cycles of creation and destruction, from which the world is produced each time.

Bhuvanesvari does not have a consort, which is unusual for female deities in the Hindu tradition. The same is true for the other Mahavidyas, although some believe that they are loosely associated with Siva, who is sometimes portrayed as the consort of the Goddess. For those who are associated with male deities such as Kali, Tara, and Kamala, the association is down-played or ignored when they are worshipped as part of the Mahavidyas. If they are depicted with male counterparts, they dominate him, most often by standing on his prone form. Bhuvanesvari is, however, associated with the formless Brahman, one of Visnu's avatars, as are all the Mahavidyas.

Bagalamukhi

Bagalamukhi Devi is the eighth of the ten Mahavidyas. 'Dasha Mahavidya' (Geeta Press, Gorakhpur) describes, "Bagalamukhi as 'The Crane-Headed One'. David Frawley terms, "Bagala is a Goddess of speech, and as such is related to Tara and regarded as a form of her. She is the power or Shakti of cruelty. She is said to be the ultimate weapon to destroy all the enemies of the universe. Mother is described as the super power which paralyses evil forces. In this sense she is the helper of Parabraham and the controller of speech, movement and knowledge. It may therefore be unfair to brand her as goddess of black power or magic. To Goddess Bagalamukhi, protection of the devotee is the inherent motive. Bagalamukhi, also known as Bagala, essemtially pertains to control, nullify or destroy the enemy.

She is considered the destroyer of internal and external adversaries and the one who aids Parasiva (the Absolute) in his cosmic function. Besides these aspects, she is also the bestower of fulfillment of all desires- worldly as well as 'bliss'. Her Pithas are located at Datia (M.P.), Varanasi (Sindhiya Ghat), Siddhaparvata (Raichur) and Gauri Pitha (Navilgund, Karnataka) and few other places. There are also individual practitioners of the Goddess all over India. Bagalamukhi is also known as Pitambari Devi, the yellow hued one. Her complexion, clothing, ornaments, and garlands are in varying shades of yellow. Her devotees are dressed in yellow, wear the rosary of turmeric and offer her yellow things. Bagalamukhi is praised as the giver of supernatural powers (siddhis) or magical powers (riddhis meaning good fortune, prosperity, wealth)

In 'Bagalamukhistotratram', a part of 'Rudrayamala' (a famous Tantra work), there are hymns in praise of the powers of Goddess Bagalamukhi –

"Vadi Mukati Rankati Kshitipatirvaishwanarah Sheetati Krodhi Samyati Durjanah Sujanati Khsipranugah Khanjati. Garvi Khanjati Sarvaviccha Jarati Tvanmantrinaamantritah Srinitye Baglamukhi Pratidinam Tubhyam Namah"

(*By the effect of Your Mantra good conversationalists become speechless; rich become beggars; devastating fire gets cooled. The anger of the angry person is removed; an evil minded person becomes good. The quick moving person becomes crippled. The conceit of the conceited person is reduced. Knowledgeable person nearly becomes a fool. Salutations to the compassionate Bagalamukhi!*)

Dhumavati

Dhumavati represents the fearsome aspect of Devi, the Hindu Divine Mother. She is often portrayed as an old, ugly widow, and is associated with things considered inauspicious and unattractive in Hinduism, such as the crow and Chaturmas period. Dhumavati personifies the destruction of the world by fire, when only smoke (dhuma) from its ashes remains. She represents the erosive power of time that robs us of loved ones, of our own youthful strength & vitality, and of whatever else contributes to our fragile happiness.The Goddesses in Hindu Dharma are often depicted as powerful and radiant. They are beautiful, celestial, with virtues such as grace,knowledge, wealth etc. One form of the Goddess is different from the rest, smoky complexioned, riding a chariot with a flag bearing a crow- Dhumavati.Seventh of the 10 Mahavidyas, Dhumavati personifies the dark side of life. Her name means "she who is made of smoke."

Iconography

Goddess Dhumavati is depicted as an old, ugly widow. She is thin, unhealthy with smoky complexion. Unlike other Mahavidya(s), she is unadorned with jewellery. She wears old, dirty clothes and has dishevelled hair and is portrayed with two hands. In one of her trembling hands, she holds a winnowing basket and makes either boon conferring gesture or knowledge giving gesture with the other hand. The boon conferring gesture and knowledge giving gesture are known as Varada Mudra and Chin Mudra respectively. She rides on a horseless chariot bearing an emblem of a crow.She is the only one of the Mahavidyas without her consort.

Dhumavati temple

Dhumavati temples are also very rare. The most famous temple of Goddess Dhumavati is located in Varanasi where the Goddess is worshipped with very unusual items. She is offered fruits, flowers along with meat, bhaang, liquor, cigarettes etc

Source: thehinduheritage

Kamala

Goddess Kamala is one of the Dasa Mahavidyas or the ten great wisdom goddesses of Hinduism. She is also known as Kamalatmika, which means "one who has a lotus in her hands." She is associated with wealth, prosperity, fertility, and abundance. In Hindu mythology, Kamala is often depicted as a beautiful, golden-skinned goddess sitting on a lotus flower. She is adorned with jewels and holds two lotus flowers in her hands, which represent purity and prosperity. Her mount is Garuda, the divine eagle.

Kamala ("she of the lotus"), is the last in the list of the Ten Mahavidyas (great revelations or manifestations), who are a group of Tantric goddesses. Kamala's place as the last of the Mahavidyas is not addressed in the literature. Although it may be taken as signifying lesser importance than the others, Kamala is one of the most widely worshipped outside of her relationship with the Mahavidyas (Kinsley 1998: 223). She is portrayed as auspicious and beautiful, with a lovely golden complexion. She is seated in a lotus posture upon a lotus flower. She has four hands—two holding lotuses and two held in signs of granting blessings and giving assurance. Iconography of Kamala illustrates her being bathed in nectar by two (sometimes four) large elephants. Kamala is represented in a similar manner to the very popular goddess Sri-Laksmi, as Kamala and Sri-Laksmi are considered to be the same goddess (Kinsley 1988; Kinsley 1998).

Kamala is also associated with the Hindu god Vishnu, who is often depicted as resting on a lotus flower. In this context, Kamala represents the creative and nurturing power of the universe, while Vishnu represents the sustaining and

preserving power. Kamala is believed to be the embodiment of the three goddesses of wealth, Lakshmi, Saraswati, and Kali. She is worshipped for blessings of wealth, success, and prosperity, as well as for fertility and the fulfillment of desires. In the Dasa Mahavidya system, Kamala represents the fifth of the ten wisdom goddesses. Each goddess in this system represents a different aspect of the divine feminine and represents a different quality or power of consciousness.

Kamala's worship involves the chanting of mantras, offering flowers and fruits, and performing pujas or rituals. Her worshippers believe that she can bestow abundance, prosperity, and material success, as well as spiritual growth and enlightenment. By invoking Kamala, they seek her blessings to overcome poverty, disease, and misfortune in their lives.

Goddess Kamala is a significant deity in Hinduism, representing wealth, prosperity, and abundance. Her worship is an important part of Hindu spiritual practice and is believed to bring blessings of material and spiritual growth to her devotees. The Mahavidyas are worshipped in temples, or in Tantric fashion (Kinsley 1998). During temple worship, rituals are performed by priests, and people may join in public worship of the goddesses. Many of the more inauspicious Mahavidyas accept blood offerings, given in the form of animal sacrifice, in addition to offerings of flowers, incense, and fruit. Worship of the Mahavidyas in temples involves conceptualization of these goddesses as existing outside, above, or beyond the worshipper, similar to the worship of other Hindu deities (Kinsley 1998: 49-50). During Tantric worship, the mantra of an individual goddess is recited repeatedly, in combination with specific hand gestures, offerings, and other details (Kinsley 1998: 49-55). Kamala is among the few Mahavidyas to have several temples across India dedicated to her as an individual goddess, as she is most often worshipped as Sri-Laksmi (Kinsley 1998: 49).

In the context of the Mahavidyas, Kamala is recognizable as Sri-Laksmi; however, there are significant differences in her character. In many ways, Laksmi's qualities appear to be altered in order to make her a better fit for the Mahavidyas (Foulston and Abbott 124; Kinsley 1998: 228-229). As a part of the Mahavidyas, Kamala remains a symbol of beauty and prosperity. She is generally still flanked by elephants, who symbolize sovereignty and fertility, maintaining Laksmi's association with these qualities. Similarly, her consistent association with the lotus maintains her representation of creative consciousness and ritual purity (Kinsley 1998: 228; Shankaranarayanan 110-111).

Matangi

The Mahavidyas have been known as a group since around the tenth century C.E (Kinsley 1). They are said to all be different expressions of the same goddess, who take on different forms for the needs of her devotees (Kinsley 2). It is said that "each Mahavidya is one facet of a multi-faceted Great Goddess and that each facet contains all the others" (Kinsley 39). Though some of the Mahavidyas are popular on their own, Matangi is rarely associated apart from the group (Kinsley 2). However, Matangi is still a unique goddess with many traits that make her powerful.Earliest traces of Matangi arise in the story from the *Divyavadana*, a Buddhist collection of stories. There is a story of a low caste girl, whose father-in-law is said to be the king of elephants. In this story, there are parallels to Matangi's power to attract and control, as well as distinct ties to nature (Kinsley 212). All these are important to Matangi as a goddess; however, they merely show hints of her characteristics, not a story of the goddess herself.

Goddess Matangi is a revered deity in the Hindu pantheon, associated with speech, knowledge, music, and the arts. Her origin and history can be traced back to ancient Indian mythology and Vedic literature.

Origin:

Goddess Matangi is believed to have originated from the goddess Parvati, who is the consort of Lord Shiva. According to Hindu mythology, Parvati assumed the form of Matangi in order to aid Lord Shiva in his battle against the demon Tarakasura. In this form, she is said to have possessed immense knowledge and the ability to control all forms of sound and speech. It is also believed that Matangi emerged from the body of the goddess Saraswati, the Hindu goddess of knowledge and the arts, who is often depicted playing the Veena.

History:

The worship of Goddess Matangi is long and varied, and she is revered in many different traditions of Hinduism. In some traditions, she is worshipped as the daughter of the god Brahma, while in others, she is seen as an incarnation of the goddess Kali. She is also closely associated with the Tantric traditions of Hinduism, where she is revered as one of the ten wisdom goddesses and is often invoked in rituals related to knowledge, creativity, and the arts.

Iconography:

Goddess Matangi is depicted as a beautiful, dark-skinned goddess with four arms. She is usually shown holding a sword, a noose, a goad, and a veena (a musical instrument). Her complexion is said to represent the dark, primordial energy of the universe, and she is often associated with the element of sound. In some depictions, Goddess Matangi is shown standing on a corpse, which represents the ego or the negative aspects of the human psyche. This

|| Shri Rajashyamala ||

symbolizes her ability to control and transform negative energies into positive ones. She is also sometimes depicted with a parrot, which represents her ability to control speech and communicate effectively.

Goddess Matangi has a rich and complex history in Hindu mythology and is revered as a powerful deity associated with knowledge, creativity, and the arts. Her iconography and symbolism are deeply rooted in Hindu tradition, and she continues to be an important figure in the worship of the Dasa Mahavidyas to this day.

Sodashi

Goddess Sodashi is one of the ten Mahavidyas or the Dasa Mahavidya group, which are ten aspects of the divine feminine in Hinduism. Sodashi is considered to be the highest form of Tripura Sundari, who is also known as Shodashi. In this essay, we will discuss the origin, iconography, temples in India, and fairs and festivals associated with the worship of Goddess Sodashi.

Origin:

The origin of the worship of Goddess Sodashi can be traced back to the Vedic period. She is mentioned in the Tripura Upanishad as one of the ten Mahavidyas. According to mythology, Sodashi was created from the combined powers of the gods Brahma, Vishnu, and Shiva. She is also considered to be the embodiment of the three goddesses - Mahakali, Mahalakshmi, and Mahasaraswati.

Iconography:

Goddess Sodashi is depicted as a beautiful young woman with sixteen arms, hence the name Sodashi which means "sixteen" in Sanskrit. She is often depicted with four arms, and each of her arms holds a different object, symbolizing her powers and attributes. The objects held by her arms include a bow and arrow, a lotus, a bell, a discus, a sword, a shield, and a trident. She is also sometimes depicted sitting on a lotus flower with a crescent moon on her forehead.

Temples in India:

There are several temples dedicated to the worship of Goddess Sodashi in India. Some of the most famous temples include the Tripura Sundari temple in Udaipur, Rajasthan, the Sodashi Temple in Guwahati, Assam, and the Tripura Sundari Temple in Agartala, Tripura. The Tripura Sundari temple in Udaipur is considered to be one of the most important temples dedicated to Sodashi.

Fairs and Festivals:

The worship of Goddess Sodashi is associated with several fairs and festivals in India. The most famous festival associated with Sodashi is the Tripura Sundari Jayanti, which is celebrated in the month of Chaitra (March-April) in the Tripura Sundari Temple in Udaipur, Rajasthan. The festival is

celebrated for three days and is attended by thousands of devotees who come to offer their prayers to the goddess. Another important festival associated with Sodashi is the Navaratri festival, which is celebrated for nine days in the month of Ashwin (September-October). During the festival, devotees worship the different forms of the divine feminine, including Sodashi. The festival is celebrated with great fervor and devotion in different parts of India.

Goddess Sodashi is an important deity in Hinduism, particularly in the worship of the divine feminine. She is considered to be the highest form of Tripura Sundari and is worshipped for her powers of strength, knowledge, and prosperity. The iconography of Sodashi and her temples in India reflect the rich cultural and religious heritage of the country. The fairs and festivals associated with the worship of Sodashi are a testament to the deep devotion and reverence of her devotees.

Kakini

Kakini is a Tantric Goddess, Yoginī, who controls the anahata-chakra or svadhishthana-chakra. She is part of the Yogini group, which embodies the forces associated with the physical substances of the body (dhatu), and with the subtle level of the chakras. In addition to Kākiī, the group includes ākinī, Rākiī, Lākiī, Śākiī, Hākiī, and sometimes Yākiī. The basic text "Rudra-yāmala", which is the source for many later tantras, contains descriptions of chakras and their inherent Goddesses, with each given her own stotra, sahasranama and practice. The treatise on chakras "acakra-nirūpaa" states about Kakini the following:

"Here dwells Kakini, who in color is yellow like unto new lightning, exhilarated and auspicious; three-eyed and the benefactress of all. She wears all kinds of ornaments, and in Her four hands She carries the noose and the skull, and makes the sign of blessing and the sign which dispels fear. Her heart is softened with the drinking of nectar."

In the svadhisthana-chakra (svādhihānāmbujagatā-504) the Goddess takes the form of Kakini (kākinīrūpadhāriī-513). She is beautiful with her four faces (caturvaktramanoharā- 505). She possesses four weapons, namely Shula, Gong, Kapala and Abhaya (śūlādyāyudhasampannā-506). She is yellow in color (pītavarā-507), incomparable (atigarvitā-508). She controls fat (medonihā-509) and prefers honey (madhuprītā-510). She is accompanied by Shakti, led by Bandhini, etc. (bandhinyādisamanvitā-511). She loves food cooked with curd (dadhyannāsaktahdayā-512).

Bhairavi

Goddess Bhairavi, also known as Bhairavi Devi is a significant deity in Hinduism and a manifestation of the Divine Feminine. She represents the fierce and powerful aspect of the goddess, associated with destruction and transformation. Often referred to asTripura- Bhairavi, she is the Goddess of the three "puras", identified by Yogis as three states of jāgrat (waking), swapna (dreaming) and sushupti (sleeping). It may also symbolize the three worlds of the material, subtle and causal, beyond which lie the fourth and powerful realm of authentic spirituality. Bhairavi, in the Mahavidyā pantheon, is that terrifying force, which destroys all obstacles in the path of a seeker, or makes him persist in these three lower and more mundane states of reality, allowing an unhindered ascension or access to the condition of Turiya or true adhaytma. Destruction, is fundamental to the path of Tantra, as evident in the eulogy offered to the Universal Divine Mother in the Chandipath with the sloka: "Srishti Sthiti Vinashanam, Shaktibhute, Sanatani"

The Tantrasarā describes 12 such forms: Sampatprada Bhairavi, Sakalasiddhi Bhairavi, Bhayavinashini Bhairavi, Chaitanya Bhairavi, Bhuvaneshwari Bhairavi, Kameshwari Bhairavi, Annapurneshwari Bhairavi, Nitya Bhairavi, Rudra Bhairavi, Bhadra Bhairavi, Subhamkari Bhairavi, and Smashana Bhairavi.

History and Evolution:

The origins of Goddess Bhairavi can be traced back to ancient Hindu scriptures and tantric traditions. She is one of the ten forms of the Divine Mother known as the

Dasa Mahavidyas. The Dasa Mahavidyas are a group of goddesses who embody different aspects of knowledge, power, and consciousness.

Iconography:

Goddess Bhairavi is depicted as fearsome, with a fierce expression on her face. She is usually shown with a dark complexion and is adorned with various ornaments, wearing a garland made of human heads, symbolizing her role as the destroyer of ignorance and ego. Bhairavi is often depicted with four arms, each holding different symbolic objects. One of her hands holds a trident (trishula), representing her power to destroy negativity and obstacles. Another hand carries a bowl or skull cup (kapala) filled with blood, symbolizing the consumption of worldly desires. The third hand holds a book or a rosary, signifying knowledge and wisdom. The fourth hand makes a gesture of fearlessness (abhaya mudra), assuring her devotees of protection.

Temples in India:

There are several temples dedicated to Goddess Bhairavi throughout India. Some of the prominent ones include:

- Chausath Yogini Temple, Morena: Located in Madhya Pradesh, this ancient temple is dedicated to the 64 Yoginis, including Bhairavi. It is believed to be one of the oldest Yogini temples in India and holds immense tantric significance.
- Baidyanath Temple, Deogarh: Situated in Jharkhand,

this temple complex houses the famous Baidyanath Jyotirlinga. It also has a shrine dedicated to Goddess Bhairavi, where devotees offer their prayers.

- Vaishno Devi Temple, Katra: This highly revered temple in Jammu and Kashmir is dedicated to Goddess Vaishno Devi, who is believed to be an incarnation of Goddess Bhairavi. Devotees often visit this temple to seek the blessings of both deities.

Fairs and Festivals:

Fairs and festivals play an essential role in the worship and celebration of Goddess Bhairavi. These events provide devotees with an opportunity to connect with the divine and seek blessings. While specific festivals dedicated solely to Bhairavi might be relatively rare, she is often worshipped during broader festivals celebrating the Divine Mother, such as Navaratri and Durga Puja. During these festivals, special rituals, prayers, and offerings are made to invoke the energy and blessings of Goddess Bhairavi. Devotees may perform elaborate ceremonies, recite hymns and mantras, and participate in processions to honour her. In contemporary times, the worship of Goddess Bhairavi continues to hold significance for many devotees. Her fierce aspect represents the power to overcome challenges, face fears, and transform oneself.

Chapter 5

Grama Devatas / Grama Devatis of Odisha

Grama devatas are village deities that are worshipped by the people of Odisha. These deities are believed to be the protectors of their respective villages and are revered by the locals. In Odisha, the Grama devatas are an integral part of the state's cultural heritage, and their worship is an important aspect of the religious practices of the people.

Durga:

Durga is a powerful and fierce deity who is worshipped as Grama devata in many villages of Odisha. She is believed to protect the village from evil spirits and negative energies. Durga is usually depicted riding a lion or a tiger and holding weapons like a trident and a sword. The most famous festival associated with Durga is Durga Puja, which is celebrated with great enthusiasm in many parts of Odisha.

In the Indian state of Odisha, the worship of deities holds immense significance and is deeply ingrained in the cultural and religious fabric of the region. Among the plethora of revered deities, Durga, the embodiment of divine feminine power, occupies a central position in the hearts and minds of the people. In Odisha, Durga is not only worshipped as Mahadevi (great goddess) in major temples but also revered as the Grama Devata (village deity) in numerous rural communities.

Temples dedicated to Durga as Grama Devata:

Throughout Odisha, one can find innumerable villages and hamlets where Durga is worshipped as the Grama Devata. These village shrines, though relatively smaller in size compared to the major temples, play a pivotal role in the spiritual and social life of the rural communities. Each village typically has its own Durga temple, which serves as a focal point for religious ceremonies, cultural celebrations, and community gatherings.

The architecture of these Grama Devata temples varies but generally follows the traditional Odia temple style. They are characterized by a main sanctum or garbhagriha, a porch or jagamohana, and sometimes additional structures like natamandira (dancing hall) or bhogamandapa (offering hall). The temples are often adorned with intricate stone carvings and sculptures depicting various manifestations of Durga and other deities.

Unique Features of Durga's Worship:

The worship of Durga as Grama Devata in Odisha is marked by distinctive rituals and practices that reflect the regional traditions and cultural heritage. Here are some notable features:

Annual Festivals: Each village celebrates an annual festival dedicated to Durga as the Grama Devata, which attracts both local devotees and visitors from neighboring areas. These festivals, known as Durga Puja or Durga Puja

Mahotsav, are usually held during the autumn season and span several days. Elaborate rituals, including arati (ritualistic offering of light), bhajans (devotional songs), and cultural performances, are performed during these festivities.

Chandi Patha: Chandi Patha, the recitation of verses from the Durga Saptashati (a sacred text praising Durga), forms an integral part of the worship. The priest or a designated devotee chants these verses, invoking the divine blessings and protection of Durga.

Bhog Offering: Devotees offer various food items and delicacies to Durga as part of the bhog (offering). This food is believed to be sanctified by the deity's divine presence and is later distributed among the devotees as prasad (blessed food). The bhog offering often includes traditional Odia dishes, such as rice, lentils, vegetables, sweets, and seasonal fruits.

Dance and Music Performances: Cultural programs, including folk dances like Gotipua, Odissi, and Ghoda Nacha, are organized during the Durga Puja festival. These performances showcase the rich artistic heritage of Odisha and add a vibrant touch to the celebrations.

Community Participation: Durga Puja as a Grama Devata festival is a community-driven event. The villagers actively participate in the preparations, decoration of the temple, and various rituals. It fosters a sense of unity and solidarity among the residents, strengthening social bonds.

Ritual Processions: During the festival, the Grama Devata temple often hosts colorful processions.

Manasa: Manasa is a serpent goddess who is worshipped as a Grama devata in many rural areas of

Odisha. She is believed to have the power to cure snake bites and protect the village from snakes and other dangerous creatures. Manasa is usually depicted as a beautiful woman with a serpent around her neck. The most famous festival associated with Manasa is Manasa Puja, which is celebrated during the monsoon season.

Saptamatrika: Saptamatrika is a group of seven goddesses who are worshipped as Grama devatas in many villages of Odisha. These goddesses are believed to have the power to protect the village from evil spirits and negative energies. The seven goddesses are Brahmani, Maheshwari, Kaumari, Vaishnavi, Varahi, Indrani, and Chamunda. They are usually depicted as beautiful women, each holding a weapon and riding a different animal.

Budhi Thakurani: Budha Thakurani is a Grama devata who is worshipped in many coastal villages of Odisha. She is believed to be the protector of fishermen and is worshipped for a good catch and safe journey at sea. Budha Thakurani is usually depicted as a beautiful woman holding a fish in her hand. The most famous festival associated with Budha Thakurani is the Bali Yatra, which is celebrated during the Kartik Purnima festival.

Kali: Kali is a powerful and fierce deity who is worshipped as a Grama devata in many villages of Odisha. She is believed to protect the village from evil spirits and negative energies. Kali is usually depicted as a black-skinned woman with long hair, wearing a garland of skulls and holding a severed head in her hand. The most famous festival associated with Kali is Kali Puja, which is celebrated during the Diwali festival.

Sitala: Sitala is a Grama devata who is worshipped in many villages of Odisha as the goddess of smallpox. She is believed to have the power to cure smallpox and protect the village from the disease. Sitala is usually depicted as a beautiful woman holding a broom in her hand. The most famous festival associated with Sitala is Sitala Sasthi, which is celebrated during the month of June.

Thakurani: Thakurani is a Grama devata who is worshipped in many villages of Odisha as the goddess of fertility. She is believed to have the power to bless the village with good harvests and prosperity.

Odisha is a state in eastern India with a rich cultural heritage, and the worship of Grama devatas or village deities is an important aspect of its religious practices. The state is divided into four regions - East, West, North, and South, each with its unique Grama devatas.

Grama Devatas of East Odisha:

Maa Anlai: Maa Anlai is a Grama devata worshipped in the coastal areas of East Odisha, especially in the Puri district. She is believed to protect the fishermen and their boats and bring prosperity to the village. She is usually depicted holding a fish in her hand. The most famous festival associated with Maa Anlai is the Bali Yatra, celebrated during the Kartik Purnima festival.

Maa Anlai, also known as Maa Anlai Chandi, is a revered deity worshipped in the coastal town of Puri, Odisha.

Worship of Maa Anlai:

Maa Anlai is worshipped with great devotion and reverence by the locals of Puri. She is considered the presiding deity of the fishermen community and is believed to bless them with a bountiful catch and protection at sea.

Iconography:

Maa Anlai is depicted as a powerful goddess, usually shown with four hands. She holds a trident (trishula) and a conch shell (shankha) in two of her hands, while the other two hands are in mudras (gestures) representing blessings and protection.

Temple:

The temple dedicated to Maa Anlai is located near the sea shore in Puri. It is a small yet significant shrine where devotees offer prayers and seek blessings from the goddess.

Annual Festival:

The worship of Maa Anlai culminates in an annual festival known as "Anlai Chandi Yatra" or "Chandana Yatra." This festival is celebrated during the month of Chaitra (March-April) and lasts for 42 days. It is one of the major festivals of Puri and attracts devotees from far and wide.

Chandana Yatra:

The Chandana Yatra begins with the construction of a wooden idol of Lord Jagannath, known as "Chandi Medha," in the Maa Anlai temple. The idol is adorned with sandalwood paste (chandana) and various decorations. A unique feature of the Chandana Yatra is the boat procession (Nauka Vihara) that takes place in the nearby Narendra Tank. The idol of Maa Anlai is taken in a beautifully decorated boat, accompanied by devotional songs and music.

During the festival, devotees enthusiastically participate in various rituals and cultural programs. They offer prayers, perform bhajans (devotional songs), and seek blessings for prosperous livelihood and safety at sea. The Chandana Yatra showcases vibrant cultural performances such as traditional dances, music recitals, and theater. These performances showcase the rich cultural heritage of Odisha and add a festive charm to the celebrations. The sandy beach of Puri becomes a canvas for renowned sand artists who create mesmerizing sculptures depicting the glory of Maa Anlai and her significance in the local folklore. The worship of Maa Anlai reflects the deep connection between the people of Puri and the sea. It symbolizes their reliance on the bounties of the ocean and their faith on the protective powers of the goddess. The festival of Maa Anlai is a testament to the strong bond between the fishing community and their patron deity.

Maa Biraja : Maa Biraja is a Grama devata worshipped in the Jajpur district of East Odisha. She is believed to have the power to cure diseases and protect the village from evil spirits. She is usually depicted riding a lion and holding weapons like a sword and a trident. The most famous festival associated with Maa Biraja is the Biraja Yatra, celebrated during the Chaitra Purnima festival. The worship of Goddess Biraja holds a profound significance in Odisha, as she is revered not only in major temples but also as the Grama Devata (village deity) in several rural communities. Goddess Biraja, also known as Goddess Viraja or Vairabi Devi, is believed to be an incarnation of Goddess Durga or Parvati. She is revered as the motherly figure and the embodiment of divine power.

Temples Dedicated to Goddess Biraja:

The most famous temple dedicated to Goddess Biraja

is the Biraja Temple in Jajpur, Odisha. This temple, also known as the "Biraja Kshetra," is one of the Shakti Peethas (sacred abodes of the Goddess) and holds immense religious significance. It is believed to be the place where the navel of Goddess Sati (an incarnation of Goddess Parvati) fell during the cosmic dance of Lord Shiva. The Biraja Temple is an architectural marvel, reflecting the rich heritage of Odisha. It follows the traditional Kalinga style of temple architecture, characterized by a towering spire (shikhara) and intricate stone carvings depicting various mythological figures and deities.

Manifestation as Grama Devata:

Apart from the Biraja Temple, Goddess Biraja is worshipped as the Grama Devata in many rural communities of Odisha. Numerous villages have their own Biraja temples, where the goddess is revered as the patron deity and the protector of the villagers.

Iconography of Goddess Biraja:

Goddess Biraja is depicted as a serene and compassionate deity, often portrayed with eight arms, symbolizing her immense power. She holds various weapons and attributes, including a trident (trishula), a conch shell (shankha), a discus (chakra), a mace (gada), a bow (dhanush), and an arrow (baana). Her multiple arms signify her ability to protect and bless her devotees.

Unique Aspects of Worship:

The worship of Goddess Biraja is characterized by several unique aspects that distinguish it from other forms of deity worship in Odisha:

Asthami Yatra: The Asthami Yatra is a grand annual festival celebrated at the Biraja Temple in Jajpur. It takes place during the month of Chaitra (March-April) and attracts a large number of devotees from all over Odisha. The festival spans over eight days and culminates in a grand procession where the goddess is taken on a chariot around the town.

Saptamatruka Worship: During the worship of Goddess Biraja, the Saptamatrukas (seven divine mothers) are also revered. These deities are considered manifestations of the goddess's power and are worshipped alongside her.

Prasad Offering: Devotees offer various food items and delicacies to Goddess Biraja as part of the bhog (offering). These offerings are considered sacred and are later distributed among the devotees as prasad.

Navarna Mantra Chanting: The Navarna Mantra, "Om Aim Hreem Kleem Chamundaye Vichche," is recited during the worship of Goddess Biraja. It is believed to invoke the blessings and protection of the goddess.

Cultural Performances: During festivals and special occasions, cultural programs such as traditional dances, music recitals, and dramatic performances are organized.

Maa Hingula: Maa Hingula is a Grama devata worshipped in the Talcher area of East Odisha. She is believed to have the power to cure diseases and protect the village from fire accidents. She is usually depicted as a beautiful woman sitting on a stone throne and holding a trident in her hand. The most famous festival associated with Maa Hingula is the Hingula Yatra, celebrated during the Chaitra Purnima festival.

Kali: Kali is a powerful and fierce deity who is worshipped as a Grama devata in many villages of East Odisha. She is believed to protect the village from evil spirits and negative energies. Kali is usually depicted as a black-skinned woman with long hair, wearing a garland of skulls and holding a severed head in her hand. The most famous festival associated with Kali is Kali Puja, which is celebrated during the Diwali festival.

Durga: Durga is a powerful and fierce deity who is worshipped as a Grama devata in many villages of East Odisha. She is believed to protect the village from evil spirits and negative energies. Durga is usually depicted riding a lion or a tiger and holding weapons like a trident and a sword. The most famous festival associated with Durga is Durga Puja, which is celebrated with great enthusiasm in many parts of Odisha.

Chandi: Chandi is a Grama devata who is worshipped in many villages of East Odisha as a powerful and fierce deity. She is believed to protect the village from evil spirits and negative energies. Chandi is usually depicted as a beautiful woman with ten arms, holding weapons like a sword, a trident, a bow, and arrows. The most famous festival associated with Chandi is the Chandi Yatra, which is celebrated during the Durga Puja festival.

Grama Devatas of West Odisha:

Maa Samaleswari: Maa Samaleswari is a Grama devata worshipped in the Sambalpur district of West Odisha. She is believed to be the mother goddess who blesses the village with good harvests and prosperity. She is usually depicted as a beautiful woman wearing a crown and holding a trident in her hand. The most famous festival associated with Maa Samaleswari is the Sital Shasthi, celebrated during the month of June.

Maa Pataneswari: Maa Pataneswari is a Grama devata worshipped in the Balangir district of West Odisha. She is believed to be the goddess of the jungle who protects the village from wild animals and brings prosperity to the farmers. She is usually depicted riding a lion and holding a bow and arrow in her hand. The most famous festival associated with Maa Pataneswari is the Pataneswari Yatra, celebrated during the month of April.

Maa Nrusinghanath: Maa Nrusinghanath is a Grama devata worshipped in the Bargarh district of West Odisha. She is believed to be the goddess who protects the village from diseases and brings good health to the people. She is usually depicted as a beautiful woman sitting on a lotus and holding a conch and a discus in her hand. The most famous festival associated with Maa Nrusinghanath is the Nrusingha Chaturdashi, celebrated during the month of May.

Grama Devatas of North Odisha:

In addition to the Grama devatas of East and West Odisha, there are also several Grama devatas in North and South Odisha. These deities are worshipped by the people of their respective regions and play an important role in their cultural and religious practices.

Maa Bhadrakali: Maa Bhadrakali is a Grama devata worshipped in the Bhadrak district of North Odisha.

Mangala: Mangala is a Grama devata who is worshipped in many villages of North Odisha as the goddess of good fortune and prosperity. She is believed to bless the village with good harvests and prosperity. Mangala is usually depicted as a beautiful woman holding a trident in her hand. The most famous festival associated with Mangala is the Mangala Yatra, which is celebrated during the month of March.

Sarala: Sarala is a Grama devata who is worshipped in many villages of North Odisha as the goddess of knowledge and learning. She is believed to bless the village with wisdom and knowledge. Sarala is usually depicted as a beautiful woman holding a book in her hand. The most famous festival associated with Sarala is the Sarala Yatra, which is celebrated during the month of October.

Budhi Thakurani: Budhi Thakurani is a Grama devata who is worshipped in many villages of North Odisha as the goddess of wisdom and intelligence. She is believed to bless the village with wisdom and intelligence. Budhi Thakurani is usually depicted as a beautiful woman holding a book in her hand. The most famous festival associated with Budhi Thakurani is the Budhi Thakurani Yatra, which is celebrated during the month of November.

Pataleswari: Pataleswari is a Grama devata who is worshipped in many villages of North Odisha as the goddess of power and strength. She is believed to bless the village with strength and power. Pataleswari is usually depicted as a beautiful woman holding a trident in her hand. The most famous festival associated with Pataleswari is the Pataleswari Yatra, which is celebrated during the month of November.

Grama Devatas of South Odisha:

Tara Tarini: Tara Tarini is a Grama devata who

is worshipped in many villages of South Odisha as the goddess of power and strength who blesses the village with strength and power. Tara Tarini is usually depicted as two sisters, holding a trident in their hands. The famous festival associated with Tara Tarini is the Tara Tarini Yatra, which is celebrated during the month of March.

Samalei: Samalei is a Grama devata who is worshipped in many villages of South Odisha as a powerful and fierce deity. She is believed to protect the village from evil spirits and negative energies. Samalei is depicted as a beautiful woman with four arms, holding weapons like a trident and a sword. The Samalei Mela, which is celebrated during the month of January extols the virtues of the goddess.

Jhadeswari: Jhadeswari is a Grama devata who is worshipped in many villages of South Odisha as the goddess of power and strength. She is believed to bless the village with strength and power. Jhadeswari is usually depicted as a beautiful woman holding a trident in her hand. The most famous festival associated with Jhadeswari is the Jhadeswari Yatra, which is celebrated during the month of October

Nagakanya: The Serpent Goddess

In the vast tapestry of Hindu mythology and iconography, Nagakanya holds a significant place as the revered goddess associated with serpents. As a grama devata (village deity) and a tantric goddess, Nagakanya has a rich history, a fascinating evolution, and unique iconography. Nagakanya's roots can be traced back to ancient Indian civilization, where serpents held immense symbolism and reverence. In Hinduism, serpents are considered divine beings, often associated with fertility, protection, and cosmic energy. The worship of serpents can be found in the Indus Valley Civilization, where artifacts depicting serpent worship have been discovered. The Nagas (serpent deities) were believed to reside in Patala, the netherworld, and played a crucial role in Hindu mythology and folklore.

Over time, the worship of Nagakanya evolved and assimilated various cultural influences. In rural areas, Nagakanya is often considered a grama devata, a local village deity associated with agricultural fertility and protection. Villagers revere her as a guardian deity, believed to bring prosperity and ward off evil forces. The serpent's association with fertility is also reflected in the Nag Panchami festival, where snakes are worshipped for a bountiful harvest.

In tantric traditions, Nagakanya occupies a prominent position as a goddess representing Kundalini energy. Kundalini, often depicted as a dormant serpent coiled at the base of the spine, represents the potential for spiritual awakening and transformation. Nagakanya is believed to awaken this dormant energy, leading to enlightenment and self-realization. Tantric rituals and practices incorporate the worship of Nagakanya to harness and channel this powerful force within oneself.

Nagakanya's iconography reflects her divine attributes and significance. She is typically depicted as a half-woman and half-serpent, adorned with jewels and holding a pot filled with elixir or immortality. The serpent's hood often crowns her head, symbolizing her association with cosmic energy and protection. The coiled serpent around her waist represents the Kundalini energy, emphasizing her role in spiritual awakening. Nagakanya's depiction as a beautiful and enchanting goddess embodies the mystique and allure associated with serpents. Nagakanya, the serpent goddess, is deeply ingrained in Hindu mythology, history, and religious practices. As a grama devata, she is revered by rural communities for her protective and fertility-related aspects. Nagakanya's timeless presence in Hinduism showcases the richness and diversity of the religious and cultural tapestry of India.

Goddess Nagakanya
Kendupatana Village, Kataka

Odisha's wonderful sculptural art, apart from depicting variety of secular and religious figures, also displays images from Naaga cult ranging from different periods and in various forms. The iconography of Naaga sculptures can be broadly divided into three categories.

Theriomorphic Form- The Naaga sculpture in its full animal shape.

Theriomorphic statues, also known as zoomorphic statues, are sculptures or artworks that depict deities or divine beings in the form of animals or animal-human hybrids. These statues are prevalent in various cultures and religions across the world, including ancient Egyptian, Greek, and Indian civilizations. In the context of Hinduism, theriomorphic statues are particularly prominent in the depiction of Naga statues found in temples. Naga statues, associated with the serpent deities or Nagas, are a common sight in Hindu temples, especially those dedicated to Lord Shiva or Lord Vishnu. These statues portray Nagas as powerful, divine beings with the ability to shape-shift between human and serpent forms. The use of theriomorphic statues in the depiction of Nagas adds a symbolic and mystical dimension to their representation.

There are different types of Naga statues found in temples, each with its unique characteristics and symbolism. Some of the notable ones include:

1. Ananta Shesha Naga: Ananta Shesha Naga is depicted as a massive serpent with multiple hoods, coiled around Lord Vishnu, who is resting on a cosmic ocean. This statue represents the eternal, infinite nature of time, as well as the protective and supporting aspect of the Nagas.

2. Vasuki Naga: Vasuki Naga is often depicted as a five-headed serpent, serving as a rope or cord in the churning of the cosmic ocean by gods and demons. This statue symbolizes the interplay of opposing forces in creation and the balance of power between the celestial beings.

3. Nagaraja: Nagaraja, the king of serpents, is portrayed as a majestic figure with a human upper body and a serpent's lower body. These statues often depict Nagaraja with a crown, multiple hoods, and adorned with jewelry. Nagaraja represents the regal and divine nature of the Nagas.

4. Nagakanya: Nagakanya statues depict the feminine aspect of the serpent deities. These statues typically show a beautiful woman's upper body and a serpent's lower body. Nagakanya is associated with fertility, protection, and the awakening of Kundalini energy.

The theriomorphic nature of these Naga statues serves several purposes. Firstly, it emphasizes the divine and mystical qualities of Nagas, who are believed to possess supernatural powers and connections to cosmic energies. Secondly, the theriomorphic form allows for the embodiment of various characteristics and attributes associated with both humans and animals. The serpentine form represents the Nagas' association with fertility, protection, and cosmic energy, while the human aspect signifies their interaction and relationship with humans. Moreover, theriomorphic statues capture the imagination and create an aura of awe and reverence. They serve as focal points for devotion and meditation, inviting worshippers to connect with the divine forces represented by the Nagas. The intricate details and craftsmanship of these statues further enhance their beauty and spiritual significance. Theriomorphic statues, including the Naga statues found in Hindu temples, depict divine beings in the form of animals or animal-human hybrids. The theriomorphic form of these statues invites devotion, meditation, and a deeper understanding of the divine forces at play in Hindu mythology and religious practices.

The anthropomorphic form of the serpent goddess holds a significant place in the rich tapestry of Hindu mythology and religious practices in India. Throughout the centuries, temples across the country have been adorned with sculptures depicting this enigmatic deity. These sculptures, their artistic and cultural significance, and

Anthromorphic Form, A serpent God/Goddess having human-like body canopied by one or several hoods of a Snake.

the enduring role of the serpent goddess in Indian religious traditions is worth exploring.

Mythological Background: The serpent goddess, often referred to as Nagini or Naga Devi, represents the primal forces of creation, preservation, and destruction. In Hindu mythology, snakes are believed to possess supernatural powers and are associated with fertility, wisdom, and protection. The anthropomorphic representation of the serpent goddess embodies these attributes, making her a revered figure in Indian religious narratives.

The sculptures of the serpent goddess in Indian temples typically depict a female figure with a serpent's lower body or multiple serpent hoods extending from her head. These sculptures exhibit exquisite craftsmanship and attention to detail, showcasing the artistic prowess of ancient Indian artisans. The serpents are often shown coiling around the goddess, symbolizing her control over the primal cosmic energies.

The serpent goddess represents the life force that pervades the universe. She is associated with fertility, protection, and the divine feminine energy. The serpent hoods denote her connection to the celestial realm and her ability to transcend earthly boundaries. The anthropomorphic form emphasizes the idea of a nurturing and powerful mother figure, capable of both creation and destruction.

The prominence of the serpent goddess in Indian culture can be traced back to ancient times. Snakes have been revered in various cultures worldwide, and India is no exception. The snake symbolizes both danger and protection, and the serpent goddess embodies these dualistic aspects. She is worshipped across different regions of India, with specific rituals and festivals dedicated to her.

The anthropomorphic form of the serpent goddess carries strong connotations of female empowerment and the divine feminine. By portraying the goddess with a serpent's lower body, these sculptures challenge traditional notions of human anatomy and blur the boundaries between human and animal. The serpent goddess serves as a potent symbol of the inherent power and strength of women, breaking free from societal norms and embracing a more primal and powerful form.

Syncretism and Regional Variations: One intriguing aspect of the serpent goddess is the regional variations in her portrayal. Different regions of India have their own interpretations and names for the goddess, showcasing the syncretism of Hinduism with local beliefs and deities. These regional variations enrich the cultural diversity and highlight the adaptability of the serpent goddess as a religious symbol.

The anthropomorphic form of the serpent goddess in Indian temples is a fascinating subject of study, blending mythology, art, and cultural significance. These sculptures offer a visual representation of the divine feminine, embracing both power and vulnerability. The serpent goddess embodies the primal forces of creation and destruction, symbolizing the interconnectedness of life and the eternal cycle of existence. Her sculptures continue to inspire awe, devotion, and contemplation, making her an integral part of the religious landscape of India.

Therio-Anthromorphic form

This is a composite type where the upper body part of

the figure is in human form and the lower part of the body is like a snake with its tail.

While the first two categories of the iconographic forms are usually noticed in early period, the Therio-Anthromorphic type has come to existence in Kalingan Temple walls from 9th/10th Century AD and continued thereafter. In the temple walls of Somavamsi or Eastern Ganga period temples, we usually see Naaga-Naagi figures as common entities. Famous temples of Mukteswar or Konark Sun Temple can be taken as prime examples. In few of the cases such figures are even worshipped as the presiding deities in Odisha.

A wonderful Naaga Kanya image is worshipped as a Grama Devati of Patapur village near Kendupatana. They worship the Goddess as Budhi Jagulei. The Grama Debati bears a very complex form having half of the body of a human and half of snake.

The small temple is newly constructed, in the middle of a rice field. A huge, ancient pond is found adjacent to the temple. The remains of the ancient temple and broken carved stone pieces are still found around the temple. This image of serpent Goddess is unique with a human body from above the waist line and the lower part, that of a snake. She is canopied by five hoods over her head and was most probably the presiding Goddess at this place. The Goddess is two handed; her right hand rests on the pedestal whereas in the left hand she holds a pot. In the lower section of the pedestal over which she sits, we find a male figure and a female figure showing respect to the Goddess. Most probably they were the King and Queen who established the shrine. The male figure has a long sword attached to his waist. The most interesting thing is the eroded inscriptions on the pedestal. The fonts are eroded, but have beenidentified as Purvi Nagari that is seen in the inscriptions of 9th/10th Century AD. The image belongs to the Somavamsi ruling period.

The Goddess of Yore

Minoan Snake Goddess:

It has been said that the image of the Snake Goddess, discovered by Sir Arthur Evans at Knossos on Crete, is one of the most frequently reproduced sculptures from antiquity. Whether or not this is true, it is certainly the case that she is a powerful and evocative image. The Snake Goddess was one of the Minoan divinities associated closely with the snake cult. She is called also Household Goddess due to her attributes of the snake, which is connected with the welfare of the Minoan household. Since the snake is also symbol of the underworld deity, the Snake Goddess has some chthonic aspects as well. She was the goddess of fertility and sexuality and her worship was connected with an orgiastic cult. Her temples were decorated with serpentine motifs. In a related Greek myth Europa, who is sometimes identified with Astarte in ancient sources, was a Phoenician princess whom Zeus abducted and carried to Crete.

Digital illustration by George Sellas

Goddess Nakei Thakurani

A Gramadebati from Somavamsi Ages

Nakei Thakurani is an ancient idol being worshipped as the Gramadebati of the village, Panchagaon situated near Lingaraj Temple on the road that connects Bhubaneswar to Jatani via Sundarapada. The Gramadebati, a ten armed Mahisamardini image of early timesis worshipped as Nakei Thakurani. An old well, some Jain sculptures and ruins of a Shiva Temple signify the presence of a religious settlement once flourishing here.

Goddess Ramachandi

Bhobara, Tangi, Khurda Odisha

There are several reflections of heritage from the villages of Odisha, mostly unrecorded in Archaeological documents, with a historical background dating back tothousands of years. Villagers worship the Goddess as Ramachandi and believe that Sri Ramachandra established this shrine. The shrine may predate 10th Century AD and may have Buddhist connections too.

Note- It is also believed that the idol is actually Buddhist Goddess Marichi. Buddhism, with its roots in ancient India, has a rich pantheon of deities and divine beings. Among them, the Buddhist Goddess Marichi holds a significant place. However, it is intriguing to observe that in the temples of Odisha, Buddhist Goddesses are worshipped and revered as Hindu goddesses.

Buddhist Goddess Marichi

Marichi, also known as Marici or Marishi-ten in Japanese Buddhism, is a prominent figure in Buddhist mythology and Tantric traditions. She is often depicted as a radiant deity with multiple arms, riding a chariot drawn by seven horses. Marichi symbolizes the dawn, the first ray of light that dispels darkness, and is associated with wisdom, illumination, and protection against negative forces. In Buddhist cosmology, she is one of the Seven Sisters or Seven Great Buddhas of the Past.

Syncretism and the Worship of Buddhist Goddesses as Hindu Goddesses in Odisha:

The worship of Buddhist goddesses as Hindu deities in the temples of Odisha can be attributed to the historical and cultural assimilation between Buddhism and Hinduism in the region. Odisha, known for its rich religious heritage, has witnessed a long history of syncretism and coexistence of multiple religioustraditions. As Buddhism declined in popularity, Hinduism assimilated many Buddhist practices, beliefs, and deities into its own fold.

The Emergence of Buddhist Goddesses as Hindu Deities in Temples of Odisha:

Over time, the worship of Buddhist goddesses, including Marichi, transitioned into the Hindu religious landscape of Odisha. These goddesses were gradually incorporated into the pantheon of Hindu deities, often assimilating their characteristics and roles with existing

Hindu goddesses. This assimilation allowed for a seamless integration of Buddhist practices and beliefs into the dominant Hindu religious framework.

Local Beliefs and Regional Variations:

The worship of Buddhist goddesses as Hindu deities in Odisha's temples also reflects the influence of local beliefs and regional variations. Odisha has a rich tradition of folk and tribal worship, where deities from different religious traditions are revered and assimilated into the local pantheon. This amalgamation has resulted in unique syncretic forms of worship, where Buddhist goddesses are worshipped alongside Hindu deities.

Continuity and Adaptability:

The worship of Buddhist goddesses as Hindu goddesses in Odisha's temples exemplifies the continuity and adaptability of religious traditions over time. It highlights the ability of religious practices to evolve and transform, absorbing elements from different traditions to meet the spiritual needs of the community. The worship of these goddesses demonstrates the harmonious coexistence of different religious identities within a pluralistic society.

Cultural Unity and Interfaith Dialogue:

The worship of Buddhist goddesses as Hindu deities in Odisha's temples promotes cultural unity and interfaith dialogue. It signifies the inclusive nature of religious practices in the region, where devotees from different backgrounds come together to offer their reverence. This syncretic form of worship fosters mutual respect and understanding among diverse religious communities.

The worship of Buddhist Goddess Marichi and other Buddhist goddesses as Hindu deities in the temples of Odisha is a testament to the historical and cultural assimilation between Buddhism and Hinduism. It reflects the continuity, adaptability, and syncretic nature of religious traditions. This practice enhances cultural unity and promotes interfaith dialogue, fostering an atmosphere of mutual respect and harmony among different religious communities.

Tentulia Ramachandi

The present day temple of Goddess 'Ramachandi' is built over the ruins of an older temple. Though the original temple had crumbled into ruins, two subsidiary temples are still to be found. The architectures of these two temples indicate their construction period to be between 8th to 10th Century AD. There are no pasting materials found to bind the stones used in these temples. Rather it is done in a 'pathara bandhei' (joining the stones) technique which is generally found in early era temples. Copper plate grants discovered from places like Talamula and Balijhari suggest that, this region used to be the 'Airabata Mandala' where the Kings of Nandodvaba dynasty ruled between 8th to 10th Century AD. The Nandodvabas were the feudatory kings of the Bhaumakaras and the temple is likely to have been built by the kings of this dynasty.

The iconogrphical features of the Goddess Ramachandi reveal that it is actually a Chamunda image from the Late Bhoumakara's era. The Devi's sculpture is remarkably fashioned with display of complete human anatomy. The Goddess has a skeletal body, sunken belly, protruding eye balls, flaming hair-do and she is riding over a dead body infested with jackals. Such Chamunda images are also found in places like Maa Dhakulei Pitha of Pratapa Nagari, Cuttack & in the State museum (recovered from Dharmasala area of Jajpur district).

Goddess Andhoti Uttarayani

Khurda, Odisha

The shrine of Goddess Uttarayani is situated at the end of the village Andhoti. The small temple is built in unique 'Kakhara' architectural style like that of Vaitala Deula in Bhubaneswar and Varahi Temple of Chaurasi. This small temple enshrines the Goddess locally worshiped as Uttarayani which is actually a 'Nagakanya' sculpture. The image is beautifully carved on a black granite stone. She has the body of a woman &the tail of a snake. A canopy of five headsof snake is depicted over the head of the Devi. Flying Vidyadhara and Apsaras are also carved on the upper part of the statue. Considering the architectural style of the temple & iconographical represeantation of the Uttarayani statue, the shrine may date back to the Eastern Ganga period.

Basuli Thakurani :

The Buddhist Goddess of Kataka City, Odisha

Thomas Eugene Donaldson's research book "Iconography of The Buddhist sculpture of Orissa" contains valuable information about several Buddhist shrines present within the city limit of Cuttack.The Solapua Maa temple at Pilgrim road have two sculptures of Amitabha and Lokesvar in a very dilapidated condition. The other place that was referred to by Donaldson was the Basuli Thakurani shrine of Bania Sahi.

A huge mass of temple fragments including Naga-nagi figures, yaksha with raised hands, erotic sculptures, amalakasilas, lotus medallions, mounted lions, broken parts of Shaktipeetha and few miniature Shiva Lingas are found under a tree. Inside the newly built temple, there are three figures of Goddess. Donaldson identified the central figure of four armed female Goddess (locally addressed as "Basuli Thakurani") as Buddhist Goddess Cunda. She is seated in Vajraparyanka with her major right hand in Varada while the uplifted arm holds a rosary. The major left hand may have held a vessel but now displays a varada. The object in the uplifted hand may originally have been a book or a tridandi but has been refashioned as a goad. She is richly ornamented and wears a tall crown with a lotus finial. The back slab is decorated with a makara torana (all these features are difficult to identify being heavily covered with clothes and crown). The image may date back to early 14th Century and iconographically could represent Dhanada Tara, Bhrukuti or the Brahmanical Parvati. Basuli Devi shrine is a true representation of Kataka's ancient heritage and also the religious culture our ancient city displays!!

Chapter 6

Malevolent Goddesses

In Indian mythology, there are several female deities and spirits who are believed to possess malevolent or fierce qualities. They are often revered and worshipped for their protective and transformative powers.

Kali:

Kali is one of the most revered malevolent female deities in Hinduism. She is primarily worshipped in Eastern India, particularly in West Bengal and Assam.

Kali is depicted with a fierce expression, dark complexion, multiple arms, and a necklace made of severed heads. Symbolically, Kali represents the destruction of ego, ignorance, and negative forces. She is associated with time, death, and transformation.

Durga:

Durga, also known as Mahishasura Mardini, is another powerful and fierce goddess worshipped throughout India, particularly during the festival of Navaratri. She is believed to have multiple forms and manifestations. As Mahishasura Mardini, she is depicted slaying the buffalo demon Mahishasura. Durga symbolizes the triumph of good over evil and represents strength, protection, and divine energy.

Chamunda:

Chamunda, also referred to as Chandi or Chamundi, is a fierce goddess worshipped in various parts of India, including Himachal Pradesh, Gujarat, and Maharashtra. She is often depicted with a skeletal form, wearing a garland of skulls and holding weapons. Chamunda is associated with battle, destruction of evil forces, and protection. She represents the ferocity required to overcome obstacles and adversity.

Bhairavi:

Bhairavi is a wrathful form of the goddess Parvati and is worshipped as a malevolent deity. She is mainly revered in the Tantric traditions of Hinduism. Bhairavi is associated with the power of transformation and represents the fierce aspect of the divine feminine. She symbolizes destruction to pave the way for new beginnings and spiritual growth.

Rudrani:

Rudrani, also known as Rudra Shakti, is the female counterpart of Lord Shiva, the destroyer in the Hindu Trinity. She is worshipped in parts of North India, particularly in Rajasthan. Rudrani is associated with destruction, chaos, and the transformative aspects of existence. Her worship signifies the recognition of both positive and negative forces in the cosmic order.

Dakini:

Dakini is a female spirit or deity found in various forms of Indian mythology, particularly in Tantric traditions. Dakinis are often depicted as wrathful and fierce figures associated with magical and transformative powers. They symbolize the intensity of spiritual practice, the breaking of boundaries, and the attainment of higher consciousness.

It is important to note that while these goddesses are considered fierce or malevolent, they are not inherently evil or negative. Their ferocity is seen as a necessary aspect of the divine order, serving as protectors and catalysts for transformation. Their worship is often associated with courage, spiritual growth, and the removal of obstacles on the path to enlightenment.

In the villages of Odisha, there are various malevolent deities that are worshipped for their protective and transformative powers. These deities are believed to possess fierce and sometimes wrathful characteristics.

Pata Dei:

Pata Dei is a female deity associated with the worship of smallpox. Villagers believe that she causes and protects against this infectious disease. Pata Dei is propitiated with offerings and rituals to seek her protection and prevent the spread of smallpox.

Sulia Dei:

Sulia Dei is a powerful and malevolent deity who is associated with disease and illness. Villagers believe that she can inflict various ailments on individuals. Rituals and offerings are made to appease Sulia Dei and seek protection from her malevolent influence.

Dharani Penu: Dharani Penu is a village deity worshipped in some regions of Odisha. She is associated with misfortune, accidents, and calamities, can cause harm and bring bad luck. Worshipping Dharani Penu is seen as a way to mitigate her malevolent influence and seek protection.

Rakta Prahari:

Rakta Prahari is a malevolent deity associated with blood-related disorders and diseases. It is believed that Rakta Prahari can cause bleeding ailments and other blood-related issues. Villagers offer prayers and perform rituals to appease Rakta Prahari and seek relief from these afflictions.

Hatapathara:

Hatapathara is a deity worshipped in some regions of Odisha. She is associated with supernatural powers and is believed to possess the ability to cause harm to individuals. Hatapathara is propitiated with offerings and rituals to avoid her malevolent influence and seek protection.

Ghanta Patua:

Ghanta Patua is a malevolent deity associated with evil spirits and possession. It is believed that Ghanta Patua can protect against and control malevolent spirits.

Rituals and offerings are performed to seek Ghanta Patua's intervention in cases of possession and spiritual afflictions.

It's important to note that the worship of these malevolent deities is deeply rooted in the local folklore, traditions, and beliefs of the villages in Odisha. While their qualities may be considered malevolent or fierce, they are often worshipped with the intention of seeking protection, averting harm, and maintaining the balance between positive and negative forces in the community

Chapter 7

Goddesses of Tribal Shamanism in Different Parts of India:
A Rich Tapestry of Divine Feminine Power

India is a land of rich cultural diversity, and tribal communities play a vital role in preserving indigenous traditions and beliefs. Within the tapestry of tribal cultures, the worship of goddesses holds a prominent place. Tribal shamanism, characterized by its connection with nature, ancestor worship, and animistic beliefs, often centers around the veneration of female deities. These goddesses embody the raw power of the divine feminine, playing crucial roles as protectors, healers, and nurturers within tribal communities.

Goddesses of Tribal Shamanism:

1. Santhals of West Bengal, Jharkhand, and Odisha: The Santhal tribe reveres the goddess **Marang Buru** as the supreme deity. She is associated with nature, fertility, and protection. The Santhals believe that Marang Buru governs all aspects of their lives and seek her blessings for a bountiful harvest and well-being.

2. Bhils of Rajasthan and Madhya Pradesh: The Bhil community worships the goddess **Ban Mata**, who

represents the nurturing aspect of motherhood and fertility. She is regarded as the protector of their villages and is associated with the well-being of children and the overall welfare of the community.

3. Gond Tribe of Madhya Pradesh, Maharashtra, and Chhattisgarh: The Gond tribe venerates the goddess **Kali Mai**, who embodies both destructive and creative forces. Kali Mai is associated with fertility, agriculture, and the protection of the community from evil spirits. Her worship involves rituals performed by tribal shamans.

4. Bodo-Kachari Tribe of Assam: The Bodo-Kachari tribe worships the goddess **Mainao**, who is considered the creator and sustainer of the universe. Mainao is associated with fertility, protection, and the well-being of the community. Rituals and offerings are made to appease her and seek her blessings.

5. Khasi and Jaintia Tribes of Meghalaya: The Khasi and Jaintia tribes venerate the goddess **Ka Blei Synshar** as the supreme deity. She is considered the mother goddess who protects the community and ensures harmony and prosperity. Her worship involves offerings and rituals performed by tribal priests.

Tribal Goddesses Worshipped in Odisha:

In the state of Odisha, various tribal communities worship a range of goddesses. Some prominent tribal goddesses worshipped in Odisha include:

1. **Samaleswari**: Worshipped by the Sambalpuri tribes, Samaleswari is considered the presiding deity of

Sambalpur. She is revered as the mother goddess and is believed to fulfill the wishes of her devotees.

2. **Thakurani**: Worshipped by the Sabar tribes, Thakurani is associated with fertility, protection, and the well-being of the community. Her worship involves elaborate rituals and festivities during the Thakurani Yatra.

3. **Budhi Thakurani**: Worshipped by the Kutia Kondh tribe, Budhi Thakurani is regarded as the goddess of wisdom and knowledge. She is believed to provide guidance and blessings to her devotees.

4. **Niyam Raja**: Worshipped by the Dongria Kondh tribe, Niyam Raja is considered the divine protector of their hills and forests. He is often accompanied by the goddesses Dharani Penu and Bada Devi.

Chapter 8

Goddess Yakshi

The Yakshi is a prominent figure in Indian mythology and religious iconography. In Hinduism, she is depicted as a benevolent nature goddess associated with fertility, vegetation, and abundance. The term "Yakshi" is derived from the Sanskrit word "Yaksha," which refers to a class of nature spirits or celestial beings. The Yakshi is often depicted as a youthful and voluptuous female figure, adorned with jewellery and flowers. She is depicted as standing or sitting, usually in a graceful posture. The Yakshi is believed to possess a divine and captivating beauty, often described as enchanting and alluring.In the state of Odisha, located in eastern India, there are numerous temples adorned with sculptures of Yakshis. These sculptures can be found in various temple complexes, particularly those dedicated to Lord Shiva.

A few notable forms and sculptures of Yakshis found in the temples of Odisha:

1. The Raja Rani Temple: Located in Bhubaneswar, the Raja Rani Temple is known for its exquisite carvings. One of the main attractions is the sculpture of a Yakshi known as **Madanika**. This sculpture showcases the beauty of a sensuous woman with a

charming smile, adorned with elaborate jewellery and holding a mirror.

2. The Mukteshwar Temple: Situated in Bhubaneswar, the Mukteshwar Temple features beautiful sculptures depicting various deities and mythical beings. Among them is the image of a Yakshi known as *Alasa Kanya*. She is portrayed in a dancing posture with her body gently swaying, emphasizing her grace and allure.

3. The Lingaraj Temple: Dedicated to Lord Shiva, the Lingaraj Temple in Bhubaneswar is renowned for its architectural grandeur and intricate carvings. Within its complex, one can find the sculpture of a Yakshi named *Ambika*. She is depicted as a seductive and enchanting figure, adorned with ornaments and holding a lotus flower.

4. The Jagannath Temple: Located in Puri, the Jagannath Temple is one of the most sacred Hindu temples in India. Within its premises, various sculptures of Yakshis can be found, often depicted as attendants of Lord Jagannath. These sculptures portray Yakshis in different poses, expressing their elegance and charm.

These are just a few examples of the different forms and sculptures of Yakshis found in the temples of Odisha. Each sculpture showcases the Yakshi's beauty and enchantment, symbolizing the divine aspects of nature and fertility within Hindu mythology.

Chapter 9

Pillar Goddesses

In Indian temple architecture, pillar Goddesses, also known as Dwara-palikas or gatekeeper deities, are prominent figures positioned on either side of the entrance gate or doorway of temples. These deities serve as guardians and protectors of the sacred space within the temple complex. They are believed to ward off evil spirits, grant blessings, and ensure the sanctity of the temple.

The pillar Goddesses are typically depicted in a standing posture, facing outwards. They are often portrayed with multiple arms, holding various weapons and symbols of power. These deities are adorned with rich ornaments and garments, representing their divine status. In addition to their protective role, pillar Goddesses are also associated with fertility, prosperity, and auspiciousness.

Some prominent pillar Goddesses found in temples across India, including those in Odisha:

1. *Dvarapalas*: Dvarapalas are the most common form of pillar Goddesses. They are depicted as fierce and powerful warriors, armed with weapons like swords, maces, and tridents. Dvarapalas guard the main entrance of the temple and are believed to protect the deity within. Their role is primarily protective, ensuring the safety and sanctity of the temple complex.

2. *Mahishasuramardini*: Mahishasura mardini, also known as Durga or Shakti, is a widely worshipped Goddess in Hinduism. She is depicted as a fierce form of the divine mother, slaying the buffalo demon Mahishasura. Mahishasuramardini is often depicted as a pillar Goddess in temple architecture, symbolizing her role as the destroyer of evil forces and protector of devotees.

3. *Chamunda*: Chamunda is a fierce and terrifying form of the Goddess Durga. She is depicted with a skeletal appearance, wearing a garland of skulls and holding weapons. Chamunda is associated with destruction and is worshipped for her power to eliminate negativity and obstacles. She is often depicted as a pillar Goddess, positioned at the temple entrance.

4. *Mahakali*: Mahakali is another fierce manifestation of the Goddess Durga. She is depicted with a dark complexion, wild hair, and multiple arms holding weapons. Mahakali is considered the supreme power and is worshipped for her ability to destroy evil and protect her devotees. In some temples, she is depicted as a pillar Goddess guarding the entrance.

In temples of Odisha, where the influence of the Kalinga architectural style is prevalent, several pillar Goddesses can be found.

1. Ekamra Kanan Temple, Bhubaneswar: At the Ekamra Kanan Temple, one can find the pillar Goddesses *Chamunda* and *Varahi* positioned at the entrance. Chamunda is associated with destruction, while Varahi is a form of the Goddess Durga,

depicted with the head of a boar. These Goddesses serve as guardians of the temple complex.

2. Konark Sun Temple, Konark: The Konark Sun Temple features various pillar sculptures, including those of *Dvarapalas*. These gatekeeper deities are portrayed as warriors armed with weapons, guarding the entrance to the temple complex.

3. Jagannath Temple, Puri: The Jagannath Temple in Puri showcases pillar sculptures of Dvarapalas at its entrance. These fierce and protective deities are positioned on either side of the doorway, symbolizing their role as guardians of Lord Jagannath and the temple premises.

These are few of the many pillar Goddesses found in temples across India, including Odisha. Their presence and significance in religious worship are associated with protection, auspiciousness, and the preservation of sacred spaces.

Chapter 10

Chausathi Yogini Shrine at Hirapur

This temple is famed to have been built by the queen Hiradevi of Brahma dynasty during 9th century AD. The wave of tantrism was at its peak then and the Bhoumakaras were ruling during that period.

The entire structure of the temple is made of a type of sandstone which was probably available locally and images are carved from chlorite. The passage into the temple in the east measures 8' in length and 2'6" in breadth. In the middle of the circular enclosure there is an open square mandap, the upper portion of which shows has been reconstructed by archeological survey of India. The mandap has openings to all our sides. While the niches in the inner enclosure contain images of Yoginis, the mandap contains the images of Bhairavas. In the Yogini cult, Siva is known as Bhairav,a guardian protector who symbolizes the powers of the Vedic Gods, Agni or Fire and Rudra or Thunder & Lightening. There are ferocious images of Katyayani in the outer circle of the temple. Katyanis were war goddesses to help Durga in her fight against Mahisasura and his allies.

64 Yogini's of Hirapur

1. Maya/ Bahurupa/Chandika

Chandika is depicted as a four armed figure standing in tribhanga pose on a corpse lying prostrate at the feet. **Tribhanga**, literally meaning breaking in three parts, consists of three bends in the body, at the neck, waist and knee; hence the body is oppositely curved at waist and neck which gives it a gentle "S" shape and is considered the most graceful and sensual of the **Odissi** dance positions. Braided hair over her head, the statue is adorned with ornaments – anklets, girdle, necklace and ear ornaments adorn most Yoginis.

2. Tara

A two armed figure, mounted on a corpse in bent knee pose. The braid of hair to the left is popularly known as Keshabandha. The strands of hair are neatly combed and arranged into various conical forms of a series of diminishing tiers and placed in position by tying up the arrangement securely. Various ornaments for the head and other ornaments like armlets, anklets, girdle necklace and kappa are found.

3. Narmada

Two armed, she stands on an elephant and wears a garland of skulls or mundamala as well as various ornaments. She holds a skull-cup like kapala near to her mouth and is believed to be drinking blood. Hair is braided to the right of her head.

4. Yamuna

Four armed, the figure stands in the pratyalidha pose. The mount is a big tortoise. Her curling hair is raised over the head known as Jatamandala. Long strands of thick hair woven into three braids are wound in circular forms and held behind on the neck like a disc or a fan. A skull-cup is seen in the upper right hand.

5. Shanti/Kanti/Laxmi/Manada

Two armed, the figure is seen standing on a full blown lotus. The braid of hair is over her head. A noticeable piece of ornament is naga keyura (armlet of naga or cobra or serpent band). She is wearing a peacock feather skirt.

6. Vriddhi/ Kriya/ Varuni

Two armed, the figure has hair braided to the left of her head. The pedestal symbolizes waves. Standing in a samabhanga pose, she is adorned with ornaments on the head and body.

7. Ajita/ Gauri / Ksemankari

Four armed, Gauri stands astride an alligator. With a chignon on top of her head, she wears girdle, necklace, armlets, anklets and various ornaments on the head and is standing in a samabhanga pose.

8. Aindri/ Indrani

Two armed, mounted on an elephant, the figure has hair braided on top of the head and various ornaments decorating the head and body. She is standing on the pratyalidha pose.

9. Varahi

Four armed with the face of boar, the figure is mounted on a buffalo. Armlets, anklets girdle necklace and kappa with mukuta and kirita adorn the statue. She holds a skull cup and bow.

10. Ratnavira/Padmabati

Two armed and fierce, Padmabati stands on the hood and body of a serpent. Her braid of hair is over her head. Adorned with garland of skulls, she holds a khadga in her right hand.

11. Ashtagriba/Vanarmukhi/Murati

The figure is four armed with a monkey face. There is a camel with a long, curled neck on the pedestal as the mount. She is standing in Dwibhanga pose.

12. Vaishanavi

Two armed and with a graceful face the statue has curly hair and sarpa mukuta over her head, apart from the usual ornaments. Garuda as the mount indicates her to be Vaishnavi.

13. Panchavarahi

This graceful figure is two-armed with beautiful braid of hair and a boar as the mount. She is standing in a Tribhanga pose with a benevolent smile on her face.

14. Vadyaroopa

This two armed figure has hair braided over her head. She stands in a dwibhanga pose on a drum and has ornament on different parts of her body.

15. Charchika

Two armed statue has mount a male figure as the mount. The male figure holds the stem of a lotus in his right hand. She is standing in a tribhanga pose.

16. Betali / Marjari

Four armed figure Betali has a fish as the mount and braided hair. A garland of skulls adds to her aura with ornaments like armlets, anklets girdle necklace and kappa. She is standing in a samabhanga pose.

17. Chinnamastaka

This four armed figure has the mount as a severed head .Braid of hair floats over her bow in her lower left hand. She is standing in a dwibhanga pose.

18. Bindhyabasini / Vrisabhanana

This statue is two armed. The mount is like a flat roofed house or cave with a gap in the middle. Her face is a ferocious buffalo head with disheveled hair know as Jatamandala.

19. Jalakamini

This two armed figure mounts on a big frog. She has strikingly beautiful waist band and attire. She is standing in a tribhanga pose.

20. Ghatabara

A two armed figure, Ghatabara mounts a lion holding an elephant over her head. She appears in a dance pose.

21. Vikarali/Kakarali

A two armed graceful figure, this statue has a dog as the vahana. Her right foot is held tightly by both hands and placed over her left thigh. It appears she is in the pose of adjusting her anklet.

22. Saraswati

Standing upon a big serpent, she is a four armed figure. The Yogini Saraswati has got moustache and appears to be twisting the same. A tumuru is slung on her shoulder.

23. Birupa

This two armed figure stands in a dwibhanga pose on a pedestal engraved with waves.

24. Kauveri

This is a two armed figure with seven ratna kalasas or ratnanidhis on the pedestal. The Ratna kalasas are balanced over a full blown lotus on which she stands. Her hair is braided to the right with mukuta and kirita over her head. She wears a bejeweled girdle apart from other ornaments.

25. Varahi/Bhalluka

This statue depicts a two armed boar faced figure with raised hair in the Jatamandala style. A padmalata is engraved on the pedestal. She wears various ornaments and holds a damru in her right hand.

26. Narasimhi / Simhamukhi

This four armed lion-faced figure has hair like the mane of a lion. She appears to be holding a pot on her hand. There are five flowers with leaves on the pedestal.

27. Biraja

A two armed graceful figure, Biraja has her braid of hair to the right, mounted on a lotus bud with leaves. She is standing in a dwibhanga pose.

28. Vikatanana

This statue is a two armed ferocious figure with protruding lips and curling matted hair over her head. She is having sarpa mukuta type of hair style.

29. Mahalaxmi

A two-armed, graceful figure on a full blown lotus, Mahalaxmi wears a garland of snakes and holds vajra and a shield in both her hands.

30. Kaumari

Kaumari is a two armed, graceful figure standing on a peacock. There is akshamala on her right arm and the usual ornaments like necklace, girdle and anklets. She stands in dwibhanga pose.

31. Mahamaya

A ten armed figure and slightly bigger then rest of the yoginis, Mahamaya is mounted on a full blown lotus. A squarish Shakti peetha is placed below her feet on the ground. She is adorned with a mukuta and kirita with a beautiful necklace, bejewelled girdle anklets and armlets. This Yogini is worshipped as the presiding deity of the shrine. The locals refer to the temple as Mahamaya temple and the ancient tank at the southern side of the temple is named as Mahamaya Pushkarini.

32. Usha/ Rati

A two armed figure with a ferocious expression on her face and raised curly hair in the Jatamandal style, this statue stands in a bent knee pose. In the pedestal there is the engraving of an archer with bow and arrow in hands and quiver on the shoulder.

33. Karkari

The mount of this two-armed yogini is a crab. With the keshabandha hair style, ear ornaments, girdle and necklace, she appears in a tribhanga pose.

34. Sarpashya / Chittala

This four-armed Yogini has the face of a snake and is embellished with various ornaments. The pedestal is broken and so the vahana cannot be seen easily. She is standing in a dwibhanga pose.

35. Yasha/ Jasa

A two armed figure with the mount as a cot with four legs, this Yogini is decorated with kirita and mukuta over her head known as jatamukuta. She is standing in a tribhanga pose.

36. Aghora / Vaivasvati

This two armed figure has a furious expression with bulging eyes. The mount is a horned goat like animal. She is standing in a dwibhanga pose.

37. Bhadrakali/ Rudrakali

Rudrakali appears as a two armed figure mounted on a cow. Her hair is spread all around her face like flame. There is a sword in her right hand . With intricately designed clothes, she stands in a samabhanga pose.

38. Vainayaki/ Ganeshani

This is a two armed, elephant faced potbelly figure with an ass as the mount. She is wearing her hair in the jata juta (knot of matted hair) or jatamukuta style.

39. Vindhyabalini

A two armed figure, standing on a rat with a beautiful braid of hair to the right of her head, Bindhyabalini holds a bow in left hand and bow string on the right and seems to be balancing the arrow. She is standing in a pratyalidha pose.

40. Abhaya / Veera Kumari

A four armed beautiful figure, mounted on a scorpion, this statue has ornaments decorating her body. Her upper hands are raised.

41. Maheshwari

Maheshwari is a four armed figure, mounted on a bull. With the keshabandha hair style, she is adorned with various ornaments and standing in a dwibhanga pose.

42. Ambika / Kamakshi

This is a four armed figure with two wheels as the mount with a mongoose below. Her hands lean against both the knee joints as she is in a bent knee pose. She is holding a damru in her upper right hand.

43. Kamayani

This Yogini is a two-armed statue with a cock as her pedestal. She is adorned with various ornaments and standing in a dwibhanga pose.

44. Ghatabari

This two armed figure is mounted on a lion in a dwibhanga pose. She has curling hair over her head with ornaments known as karanda mukuta.

45. Stutee

This yogini statue is a four armed figure mounted on a haldi kathua. (Pot to keep turmeric paste). A flower vase is also engraved on the pedestal. Braid of hair is to the right with flower garlands adorned with various ornaments and mukuta. She is standing in the samabhanga pose.

46. Kali

This is a two armed figure mounted on a male body, holding a trident. The male figure is wearing mukuta and kirita and has a third eye, identified to be lord Shiva. She is standing in a dwibhanga pose.

47. Uma

Uma is a graceful, four armed figure with mukuta and kirita /jata mukuta over her head, holding a "naga phasha" in her upper left hand with the lower left arm is in abhaya mudra. Lotus flowers constitute her mount.

48. Narayani

A two armed graceful figure, Narayani has her left hand upon a madya bhanda (wine keg) and holds a sword in the right hand. With a kesha bandha hair style, she has various ornaments as her decorations. The pedestal is an earthen pot having a conical lid.

49. Samudra

A two armed figure with the braid of hair to the left, a tiara on her head and various ornaments on her body Samudra has a conch shell with two legs as the mount. She is standing in a dwibhanga pose.

50. Brahmani

This four armed and three faced figure, with kirti and mukuta or jata and sacred thread and ornaments adorning her body, Brahmani has a book as the mount. At the left end of the pedestal a majestic lion is carved with beads in its mouth.

51. Jwalamukhi

A two armed figure mounted on a platform with eight legs, her ears are raised and long. Two long knots of matted hair are found hanging on both sides of her head. She stands in a dwibhanga pose.

52. Agnihotri / Agneyi

Two armed figure standing on a ram, this Yogini holds a sword in the raised right hand. She is adorned with various ornaments. The flames of fire surround her.

53. Aditi

Two armed with a chignon on top, Aditi has a parrot on the pedestal as the mount She stands in a samabhanga pose.

54. Chandrakanti

Two armed figure mounted on wooden cot with four legs, this staute wears her hair in the Keshabandha style along with various ornaments. She stands in a dwibhanga pose.

55. Vayubega

A two armed graceful figure, with a chignon over her head, Vayubega has a female yak as her mount.

56. Chamunda

This four armed awe-inspiring figure, with a skeletal body and dangling breasts, Chamunda is wearing a garland of skulls. She holds a lion hide over her head. In the lower two hands she holds a katari and a severed human head. The musk deer is the mount of this ferocious yogini standing in the tribhanga pose.

57. Murati

Murati is a two armed figure mounted on a horned deer and the braid of hair spread out like flames. Bejewelled with various ornaments she stands in tribhanga pose.

58. Ganga

A four armed figure standing upon the back of Makara , she is adorned with various ornaments. She holds the stalk of a full blown lotus in her upper right hand and a naga phasha in her lower left. She is standing in a tribhanga pose.

59. Dhumavati / Tarini

This two armed figure is mounted on a duck. She holds a fan in both her hands and stands in a samabhanga pose.

60. Gandhari

A two armed figure mounted on a horse, this statue has a kadamba tree in the background. She stands in a samabhanga pose.

61. Ajita

This four armed figure has hair style appearing like flames. There is a stag on the pedestal as the mount. She stands in a tribhanga pose.

62. Surya Putri

She is a four armed figure and graceful in appearance. She is mounted on a galloping horse. With kirita on head and various ornaments adorning her body. She holds a bow and arrow with a quiver.

63. Vayu Veena

This two armed has hair braided to the right of her head. Adorned with various ornaments and intricate earrings known as kappa, she appears resplendent on a pedestal with an engraving of a black buck and two flower vases.

64. Sarva Mangala

This is the missing Yogini with an empty niche. The statue of sarva mangala was housed here.

The Hirapur Yoginis are extraordinarily beautiful figures with exquisitely carved features and sensuously formed bodies. They are standing figures with elaborate ornaments of various types. A gentle maiden adjusting an anklet, exudes femininity and sensuality with her softly curved stomach, wide hips and elegant posture. Her slim, flexible figure is admirably portrayed, while her eyes, eyebrows and lips have delicate lines. The ornaments are highly ornate- the bracelets, armlets, necklaces, anklets, earrings, garland and the headdress. The hairstyles are also either a one sided bun or a coronet of interlocking curls.

Chapter 11

The Chausathi Yoginis of Ranipur Jharial

The Chausathi Yogini temple at Ranipur Jharial is one of the two hypaethral temples of Odisha, (the other temple is located at Hirapur, near Bhubaneswar) significant with regard to its antiquity as well as its representation of the lost Tantra cult. By popular notion, it is believed that the hypaethral temples were constructed in dedication to deities of nature symbolizing fertility of the soil, of animals and of man.

The structure of this hypaethral temple is distinct from the Brahmanical or Buddhist temple structures. The temple is devoid of vimana or sikhara, mandapa or chambers, garbhagriha or sanctum. Locally the Chausathi Yogini temple of Ranipur-Jaharial is popularly referred to as 'Chakhar Badha' due to its circular shape.

A unique aspect of the Yogini statues at Ranipur Jharial is that all of them are dancing Yoginis, in different poses of the classical Odissi dance form, originating from Odisha. The theoretical foundations of Odissi can be traced to the ancient Sanskrit text Natya Shastra, its existence in antiquity evidenced by the dance poses in the sculptures of Hindu temples in Odisha, and archaeological sites of Hinduism, Buddhism and Jainism. The statues in temples mostly show the *Samapada*, the *Tribhangi* and the *Chauka* of Odissi. The Ranipur Yoginis are all in the Samabhanga pose and show the "Bhangas" or body positions.

The inventory of the existing Yogini statues at Ranipur Jharial temple and details of vacant niches are provided here. Researchers have tried to name them by comparing them to descriptions in ancient, sacred texts and tantric literature and drawing similarities. References about the Chausathi Yoginis can be found in ancient scriptures like : Brahmananda Purana, Agni Purana, Skanda Purana, Kalika Purana, Jnanarnava Tantra, Brihad Nandikeswara Purana, Chandi Purana of Sarala Das, Brihndla Tantra, Bata Avakasa of Balaram Das, etc. Historical romances and semi-historical literature like Somadevasuri's Yasastilaka of AD 959, Kalhana's Rajatarangini of c.1150 and Somadeva's Kathasarit Sagara of c.1070 contain legendary stories about the all-powerful Yoginis.

An attempt has been made to name the Yogini statues, in keeping with their iconography and drawing similarities with the following existing lists:

Kalika Purana, Durgapuja Paddhati of Vrihannandikesvara Purana and Brihannila Tantra, Dr. Ramprasad Mishra research article.

1. Brahmi

(*Kalika Purana, Durgapuja Paddhati of Vrihannandikesvara Purana and Brihannila Tantra*)

A three headed two armed figure, she holds a trident on her left hand and a kumbha/kamandalu on her right hand, resting on her left knee. It is probably the image of Brahmi or Brahmani, the Shakti of Brahma who according to Devi Mahatmya of Markandeya Purana has the swan as her vehicle and holds a kamandalu and aksasutra. She is a four-faced goddess, but her image here shows three faces because in accordance with the iconography of this deity one of her faces remains at the back.

2. Vacant

Belgar mentioned about the image that had originally been in this niche as "A two armed figure with a lotus in each hand, dancing on the pedestal of seven horses". *Cunningham describes her, more than a century ago as a unique statue with resemblance to the attributes of Surya, as holding a lotus in each of her two hands and as having seven horses depicted against her pedestal. (Dehejia, Yogini Cult and Temple- A Tantric Tradition.)*

3. Vacant

This niche had contained a two-armed figure, one hand holding a mace.

4. Vidyutprabha

(Skanda Purana, Prabhasvara-Yoga-Varttika)

This is a two-armed figure, single headed with her left hand on her naval in a typical posture of Odissi dance form, the right arm broken. It may be identified as the image of the Yogini Vidyutprabha who according to Tantric belief, illumines her body and invigorates her energy from her Navel-Plexus or Manipuraka Chakra.

5. Simhamukhi

(*Skandapurana and Tantric literature*)

She is a two armed lion headed figure, carrying a trident on her right hand and a cup in her left hand. It is possibly the image of Simhamuhki, whose description as a Yogini is found in Skandapurana and Tantric literature.

6. Vrihatkusi

(*Skanda Purana*) : A two armed figure, holding a noose in her left hand, and a sword in her right hand. This image Vrihatkusi, as mentioned in the Skanda Purana.

7. A four-armed figure with all hands broken.

8. Vacant

9. Vacant

10. Vacant

11. A two armed figure, left hand on her left knee, right hand broken. This Yogini is described in *Vrihat Nila Tantra* and *Sadabhichara Prayoganama Tantravallari*.

12. Maheswari

A three headed, four-armed figure. Upper right hand holds a trident and lower right hand is damaged. Upper left hand holds the rosary and lower left hand has been damaged.

13. Sukodari (*Skanda Purana*)

A skeletal figure, right arm damaged, left arm on her cheek. As the image shows a shrinking belly, it may be assumed to be the image of Sukodari who is depicted in Skandapurana.

14. Vacant

15. A broken image (Belgar mentions it in niche number 14, and describes): "A six or eight armed image; with one pair of hands she is pulling her mouth wide, and with the remaining unbroken ones she holds an hour glass, a sword, a cup, and is dancing on a prostrate male figure". Cunnigham corroborates this observation.

Her gesture of opening her mouth wide indicates that she could be Yogini Attahasa, (the one who laughs loudly) or Yogini Hahavara (the one who utters loud sounds). It is presumed that it could be the image of Devi Parvati, the MahaYogini as its height and width is comparatively more compared to other Yoginis. It may have been placed in this niche at a later date after reshuffling of images in the cells. It is probable that this Parvati image was in front of Lord Shiva near the entrance.

16. Bidali Devi

Four armed figure with the head of a cat. The Yogini holds a club and sword in two hands, a skull-cap and a piece of flesh in the other two. This image is similar to Yogini Bidalidevi, meaning cat.

17. Hayagrva (*Skandapurana*)

A horse headed figure, four armed, she holds in her unbroken hands a club, an hour glass and a rosary.

18. Ajasya Ajalochana

(*Pashu Prakashana Tantra*)

A goat-faced, four-armed image, holding a club in her left hand.

19. Vikatanana Vyaghrani

(*Skandapurana & Chausathi Yogini Namavali*)

A tiger headed, four-armed figure, carrying a bow (broken) in her upper left hand; in the upper right hand she holds an arrow and in the lower right hand a club. The lower left hand is broken.

20. Dhumanisvasa (*Skanda Purana*)

A four armed deity, two hands folded on her chest, and the other two hands broken. It is probably the image of Yogini Dhumanisvasa who exhales smoke by pressing her chest with two hands and hypnotizes the victim by magical smoke. It is a war goddess and described as Yogini in the Skanda Purana.

21. Marjari (*Skandapurana*)

A cat/leopard headed figure, four-armed; she is holding a sword in the upper right hand, and a human corpse by its legs with one of her left hands.

22. Gajananaa/Vainayaki

(*Skandapurana & Chaunsth Yogini Namavali*)

An elephant headed, four-armed figure, holding a battle axe in her upper left hand. The other hands are broken. The battle axe (symbolic of Ganesha) and elephant head connote that she could be Gajanana or Vainayaki.

23. Varahi

(*Skanda Purana, Chuansath Yogini Namavali and Brihat Nandikesvara Purana*)

A boar headed, four armed figure. With her upper right hand is carrying a club, and upper left hand, a rosary or mala. Adorned with a crown of a coiled snake, her other two hands are folded together in a Odissi dance mudra.

24. **Vrisanana** (*Skandapurana*)

A bull headed, horned, four armed figure, with all hands broken.

25. A four armed figure, she has her upper right hand on her knee. Upper left hand lies on her breast. With her lower right hand she is holding a club and with lower left hand, a cup.

26. A four armed figure; the upper left hand is on her left ankle and lower left hand holds a rosary. The upper right hand is damaged.

27. **Riksasi** (*Skandapurana*)

A four armed figure, all arms broken.

28. **Sarpasya**

(*Skandapurana*)

A serpent headed, four armed figure, one hand on her knee, another at her breast, the others holding a cup and a trident.

29. A two armed defaced figure with hands damaged.

30. A two armed figure, carrying a trident in her right hand, left hand damaged.

31. A two armed figure, with a distinct coiffure and traces of head jewellery. She has a benign expression.

32. Missing

33. **Prachanda**

(*Skanda Purana*)

A two armed figure, holding a trident in her right hand, left hand damaged.

34. Chhanda

(*Brihat Nila Tantra, Kalika Purana*)

A two armed figure holding a cup in her left hand, right hand damaged.

35. Chandanayika

(*Kalika Purana, Brihat Nila tantra*)

A two armed figure holding a trident in her right hand and a cup in her left hand.

36. A two armed figure with both the hands broken.

37. Chandogra

(*Kalika Purana, Brihat Nila Tantra*)

A two armed figure carrying a trident in the right hand and a cup in her left hand.

38. **Ksemankari** (*Kalika Purana*)

A four armed figure, carrying a trident in her upper right hand, a sword in upper left hand, with the lower left hand holding a cup. Closer scrutiny reveals a grotesque face, with sunken eyes and her hair decorated with a crown of skulls. It is probably the image of Ksemankari who is described as a Yogini in Kalika Purana.(Source: manuscript No. 345 of Odisha State Museum Library).

39. A two armed figure; both hands of this statue are damaged.

40. Vacant

41. Vacant

Forgotten Goddesses | 213

42. A stout two armed figure, holding a trident in her right hand. The left hand is broken.

43. Sisighani (*Skandapurana*)

A two armed figure, holding a sword in the right hand and having a child on her knee.

44. Sarabhanana (*Skanda Purana*)

A horse headed image of a four armed female. She holds a trident in one upper hand and a severed head by its hair in both lower hands.

45. Pasahasta (*Skanda Purana*)

Yamaghanta (*Chaunsath Yogini Namavali*)

A two armed buffalo faced figure, holding a trident in her right hand, left hand damaged. It is probably the image of the Yogini Pasahasta or the arrester of the Jiva or life,

46. Adya (*Brihat Nila Tantra*)
Yogesvari (*Chaunsath Yogini Namavali*)
Brahma Vadini (*Brihat Nandikesvara Purana*)

A four armed figure, with the upper two hands joined over her head and lower two hands joined near her naval in a dancing posture. The figure is a symbolic indication of the yogic energisation of the naval plexus/ MANIPURAKA CHAKRA and SAHASRARA CHAKRA/ Cerebral plexus by using hands.

47. Mrigasirsa(*Skandapurana*):

Deer faced, two armed figure. On her right hand she holds a sword.

48. Kotarinasika (*Skanda Purana*):

A two armed figure, holding a trident in her right hand, left hand damaged. The nose is slightly shrunk inwards, thus the name.

49. Stulakeshi (*Skanda Purana*)

A two armed figure, her right hand is in the Abhaya mudra and left hand is on her knee. The deity has thick hair carved on her head.

50. Vacant

51. Dantesukara (*Skanda Purana*)

This is a two armed figure in a distinct posture; she is rubbing her teeth with a finger of one of her hands as a toothbrush; the other holds what may be either a mirror or a cup.

52. Sreshthini

(*Chaunsath Yogini Namavali*)

A two armed figure, holding a club in her left hand. It is probably the icon of Sreshthini who confers affluence on the Sreshthins or the merchant class.

53. Vacant

54. Bhayankari

(*Brihat Nila Tantra*)

A four armed figure. Upper right hand holds a club. Lower left hand is broken.

55. Indrani

A four armed figure. Upper left hand holds a bow, upper right hand an arrow. Lower left hand holds a parasol and the lower right hand is damaged.

56. A two armed figure, holding a pair of pincers in the left hand; right hand is damaged.

57. A two armed figure, holding a noose in the right hand.

58. Vacant

59. Vala Pramathini (*Skanda Purana*)

A two armed figure, holding a club in right hand and a cup in the left hand. It is the image of Vala Pramathini whose weapons are noose and skull cup.

60. A two armed figure, one hand raised to her forehead. In the left hand she is holding a mirror. This is a typical dance pose of Odissi.

61. Dandahasta (*Skanda Purana*)

A two armed figure, right hand holding a club.

References:

1. Ellwood, Robert S. (2007). *The Encyclopedia of World Religions (Rev. ed.).* New York: Facts on File. p. 181. ISBN 978-1438110387.

2. Wolkstein, Diane; Kramer, Samuel Noah (1983). *Inanna: Queen of Heaven and Earth: Her Stories and Hymns from Sumer.* New York City, New York: Harper&Row Publishers. p. xviii. ISBN 0-06-090854-8.

3. Sylvia Brinton Perera, *Descent to the Goddess* (Toronto 1982) re Inanna and Ereshkigal.

4. Nemet-Nejat, Karen Rhea (1998). *Daily Life in Ancient Mesopotamia. Daily Life.* Greenwood. p. 182. ISBN 978-0313294976.

5. Collins, Paul (1994). "The Sumerian Goddess Inanna (3400-2200 BC)". *Papers of from the Institute of Archaeology.* Vol. 5. UCL. pp. 110–111.

6. Taheri, Sadreddin (2014). "Goddesses in Iranian Culture and Mythology". Tehran: Roshangaran va Motale'at-e Zanan Publications.

7. Wood, Juliette (2001). *The Celts: Life, Myth, and Art (New ed.).* London: Duncard Baird Publishers. p. 42. ISBN 9781903296264.

8. Mbiti, John S. (1991). *Introduction to African Religion (2nd rev. ed.).* Oxford, England: Heinemann Educational Books. p. 53. ISBN 9780435940027.

9. Chang, Jung (2003). *Wild Swans: Three Daughters of China (reprint ed.).* New York: Simon and Schuster. p. 429. ISBN 1439106495. Retrieved 22 April 2016.

10. *"Amaterasu"*. World History Encyclopedia. Retrieved 21 February 2019.

11. Kinsley, David (1988). *Hindu Goddesses: Visions of the Divine Feminine in the Hindu Religious Tradition (1st ed.)*. Berkeley: University of California Press. p. 1. ISBN 9780520908833. Retrieved 22 April 2016. goddess.

12. Bhattacharyya, Narendra (1977) *The Indian Mother Goddess*. Delhi: Manohar Book Service.

13. Donaldson, Thomas (2002) *Tantra and Sakta Art of Orissa*. New Delhi: D.K. Printworld.

14. Hawley, John & Wulff, Donna (1996) *Devi: Goddesses of India*. Berkeley: University of California Press.

15. Kinsley, David (1997) *Tantric Visions of the Devine Feminine: The Ten Mahavidyans*. Delhi: Motilal Banarsidass Publishers.

16. Pitchman, Tracy (1994) *The Rise of the Goddess in the Hindu Tradition*. Albany: State University of New York Press.

17. Prakashan, Rekha (1980) *The Little Goddesses (Matrikas)*. New Delhi: Caxton Press.

18. Rodrigues, Hillary Peter (2003) *Ritual Worship of the Great Goddess: The Liturgy of the Durga Puja with Interpretations*. Albany: State University of New York Press.

19. Samuel, Geoffrey (2005) *Tantric Revisionings: New Understandings of Tibetan Buddhism and Indian Religion*. Delhi: Motilal Banarsidass Publishers.

20. Tewari, Naren (1988) *The Mother Goddess Vaishno Devi*. Delhi: Lancer International.

Black Eagle Books

www.blackeaglebooks.org
info@blackeaglebooks.org

Black Eagle Books, an independent publisher, was founded as a nonprofit organization in April, 2019. It is our mission to connect and engage the Indian diaspora and the world at large with the best of works of world literature published on a collaborative platform, with special emphasis on foregrounding Contemporary Classics and New Writing.

www.ingramcontent.com/pod-product-compliance
Lightning Source LLC
Chambersburg PA
CBHW052137070526
44585CB00017B/1869